The Complete Guides to Horses and Ponies

My Pony

HORSE&PONY CARE

Jackie Budd

Gareth Stevens Publishing
MILWAUKEE

For a free color catalog describing Gareth Stevens Publishing's list of high-quality books and multimedia programs, call 1-800-542-2595 (USA) or 1-800-461-9120 (Canada). Gareth Stevens Publishing's Fax: (414) 225-0377. See our catalog, too, on the World Wide Web: http://gsinc.com

Library of Congress Cataloging-in-Publication Data available upon request from the publisher. Fax (414) 225-0377 for the attention of the Publishing Records Department.

ISBN 0-8368-2047-9

First published in North America in 1998 by
Gareth Stevens Publishing
*1555 North RiverCenter Drive, Suite 201
Milwaukee, WI 53212 USA*

This U.S. edition © 1998 by Gareth Stevens, Inc. Created with original © 1996 by Ringpress Books Ltd. and Jackie Budd, P. O. Box 8, Lydney, Gloucestershire, United Kingdom, GL15 6YD, in association with Horse & Pony Magazine. All photographs courtesy of Horse & Pony Magazine. Additional end matter © 1998 Gareth Stevens, Inc.

The publisher would like to thank Kate Considine, an experienced rider and trainer, for her assistance with the accuracy of the text. Ms. Considine showed in Switzerland for 2-1/2 years and has worked with Olympians from the USA. Currently, she is showing and training hunters and jumpers in the United States.

Printed in Mexico

1 2 3 4 5 6 7 8 9 02 01 00 99 98

CONTENTS

LIVING outdoors is the most natural way of life for a pony. Most ponies would prefer to be out in the field, where they can get plenty of fresh air, exercise, and free access to food in the company of their friends, rather than be confined to a stable. Even so, it is not a case of "any field will do." For a field-kept pony to stay happy and healthy, his home must be safe and suitable to live in.

Check List

EVERY field must have a constant supply of clean, fresh water. Ideally, this will come from the water line to a trough. The trough should not have sharp corners or edges. Some fields may have a stream, but the water might not be safe to drink. Mucky ponds are a danger to ponies and need to be fenced off. If there's no piped-in water, haul a large container or buckets. But remember, ponies drink up to 10 gallons (36 liters) of water a day!

IN the wild, ponies can always find a place to get out of the cold, wind, and rain. They can take cover from flies and the hot Sun. Make sure your field has shelter like this. It can be natural shelter from a large tree or hedge, or, best of all, a specially built shed. The shelter must be roomy enough for all the occupants to use, and it must have clean, dry bedding inside. Position the shed away from the prevailing wind on a high, well-drained spot.

MOST of the year, your pony will be living off the grass beneath his feet, so the pasture must have reasonable feed value. Ponies do not want rich pasture as this can make them ill. However, the field should not be bare, boggy, bitter, or full of weeds. There must be plenty of space and grass for the number of ponies living there. Allow at least 1.5 acres (6,000 square meters) of pasture per pony — a little more if the grazing is of poor quality.

Field Care Tips

PONIES are fussy grazers that tend to eat the tastiest grass and leave the rest. Good grass soon gets overgrazed and becomes bitter, while the poorer patches and toilet areas are left to get overgrown. To keep the field in good condition:

◆ **PICK up all the droppings at least once a week.**

◆ **DIVIDE the field into sections, so part of the pasture can be regularly rested.**

◆ **SEE if the field can be grazed for a while by other livestock, such as sheep or cattle.**

◆ **ASK the field owner about mowing the overgrown areas and naturally fertilizing and chaining off the pasture every so often.**

ALTHOUGH ponies can adapt to living by themselves, they are naturally sociable animals. They would be very lonely on their own. Choose a field with space for at least one friend, preferably another horse or pony.

styles

✓ **Good grazing**
✓ **Company**
✓ **Fencing**
✓ **Gate**
✓ **Water**
✓ **Shelter**

Fencing — right and wrong ways

PONIES can be incredibly accident-prone, and they are also brilliant escape artists! Rickety, low, or unsafe fencing is asking for trouble. A sagging barbed-wire fence could cause a serious injury. The best types of fencing are post and rail, or a thick hedge. Plain wire can be used, but it must be kept taut. Remember to check the fencing regularly. Repairs should be done immediately.

The wrong way (above) *could cause injury. Secure, safe wood fencing* (right).

YOUR field needs a sturdy, well-hung gate that is wide enough to lead your pony through safely, and that has a secure fastener. Ponies tend to crowd around a gate, and squabbles can develop. So gates are best positioned away from a corner and in a well-drained position. It is safest if the gate does not open onto a road.

From left: *oak, ragwort, yew, and dock.*

BEWARE

CHECK your field for plants that might be harmful to your pony. If you spot any, dig them up and burn them away from the field. The most common is ragwort that flowers in late summer. Other plants that are poisonous to ponies include yew, laburnum, and many garden shrubs. Watch out for laurel, privet, rhododendron, henbane, hemlock, foxglove, horsetail, ground ivy, buttercups (in large amounts), and oak (mainly fallen acorns). Some weeds, such as nettles, docks, and thistles, do no harm but indicate that the pasture is poor. If your field is surrounded by houses, watch for gardeners throwing lawn clippings and other items over the fence — these can give your pony a stomachache.

Indoor Life

IN the past, horses were often tied up in stalls so that many could be kept in a small area.

Today, horses are given a chance to move around in an individual stall that could be inside a large barn. Barns may be made of brick, stone, concrete blocks, or strong timber, but they must be properly built or your pony's health could be affected.

Home, Sweet Home

MANY ponies can live outside happily all year round in a good field with plenty of shelter, with extra feed in winter, and, perhaps, the help of an outdoor blanket in bitter weather. Hardy, native types are well equipped to cope with life outdoors. Other kinds of ponies — particularly those that are part Thoroughbred or part Arabian — have thinner skins and coats and do not cope well in cold, wet weather. During the winter months, they will definitely need to wear blankets and come inside to a warm stable at night.

However, horses were not designed to live indoors for long periods, and they do not like being kept in a stable all day, every day. Keeping a pony stabled full-time might make him easier to care for in some ways because he will stay clean and be on hand whenever you want to ride. But

a fully stabled pony is a big responsibility as he relies on you for his every need. This is a very time-consuming prospect. Besides all your stable chores, you will have to put aside several hours every day to ride. Ponies confined for too long become bored and unhappy and can develop health and behavior problems. It is much better to use a combined system where your pony can be turned out in a field for daily exercise in winter and stay out all the time in summer.

Having a stable is useful even for field-kept ponies because the ponies may become ill or injured outside. It is also wise to restrict a greedy pony's grazing at times.

styles

Check List

VENTILATION: Ponies need plenty of fresh air but dislike drafts. Every stable should have a window that is protected or made of reinforced glass, preferably opening inward at the top. There should be ventilation in the roof, too. Always leave the top door of a stall open.

SPACE: The bigger, the better! The minimum measurements are 10 x 10 feet (3 x 3 m) for a pony and 12 x 12 feet (3.75 x 3.75 m) for a horse. The ceiling should be at least 10 feet (3 m) high.

FLOOR: Most stables have concrete floors. These are not ideal but will do if they are sloped slightly to allow for drainage. The bedding must be kept clean.

DOOR: A sturdy door that is at least 4 feet (1.25 m) wide and 7.5 feet (2.2 m) high is necessary, so the horse or pony does not bang his head or sides.

HARDWARE: Avoid too much hardware as it will only get in the way and might hurt your pony. There may be a feed bucket that should be around chest height and blocked in so the pony cannot get trapped underneath when he lies down. A hay rack should be at your pony's nose-height. Some stables have automatic waterers, but, usually, you will need to place a large bucket in one corner by the door. Light fixtures and switches must be well out of reach. They should be the covered type.

Types of stables

UNLESS you have a stable and field at home, you will be renting a stable. There are several types from which to choose:

GRASS STABLE: The cheapest way of keeping a pony, where you simply rent a field. It is suitable only for the hardier kinds of ponies.

DIY (Do-It-Yourself): You rent a stable and, preferably, the use of a field, too. Inexpensive, but you need to look after all your pony's needs yourself.

PART STABLE: You pay a little extra for the yard owner to do some tasks, like turning out and feeding. This is ideal because it lessens your workload, and help and advice are always on hand.

WORKING STABLE: Your pony is kept at a riding school. He is used by the school and mainly cared for by the staff in return for a discounted fee.

FULL STABLE: The pony is completely looked after and exercised by the staff, although you ride when you want. Expensive — and you are missing half the fun!

Daily

DEPENDING on how you keep your pony — whether he is always outside or comes in at night, whether he is on DIY or you have some help — you need to establish a daily routine.

You must make sure that he is well looked after. But also make sure this work fits in with your school schedule and the times when an adult can drive you to the stable.

Summer checklist

MORNING AND EVENING:

◆ Catch your pony and check him over. Check the field for problems. Make sure there is water in the trough.

◆ Pick out your pony's feet.

◆ Apply fly repellent if needed. Feed him if he's been working hard.

◆ Bring your pony in for part of the day if his grazing needs to be restricted.

ONCE A WEEK:

◆ Thoroughly check fencing.

◆ Pick up droppings.

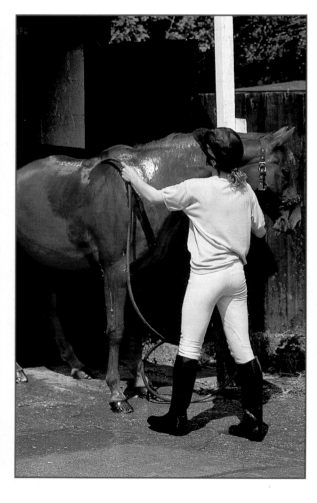

Summer Tips

◆ **Flies** can make ponies miserable in summer. Put plenty of fly repellent on your pony, or bring him into the shade of a stable or shelter in the hottest part of the day. A fly hat can help.

◆ After a sweaty ride, your pony will love a sponge bath or a hosing down. Be careful how you use a hose — he may be frightened at first.

◆ Don't ride your pony aggressively when the ground is hard. It could make him lame.

Routines

Always try to stick to a timetable. Horses soon get to know when to expect a visit, so it is not only unkind but even harmful to keep changing the times you come each day. Your routine will be slightly different in summer than winter because there are many more tasks in winter.

But, all year round, whatever the weather and whether he lives in or out, your pony needs to be visited at least twice a day.

Here are the essential things you will need to do at each visit, apart from riding. You may need to arrange help from someone else, too — perhaps another pony-owning friend or the barn owner.

Winter checklist

STABLED AT NIGHT

◆ **Morning:** Ride first, if you have time. Feed him. Pick out feet. Put on an outdoor blanket, and turn your pony out in field. Clean the stable (this can be done in the evening if you wish). Fill haynet or hay rack. Clean and refill water buckets.

◆ **Evening:** Clean the stable and take care of water and hay if not done earlier. Catch your pony. Give light grooming, and pick out feet. Ride, if you have time. Put on stable blanket. Feed.

◆ **Once a week:** Tidy the manure pile.

FIELD-KEPT

◆ **Morning AND evening:** Catch your pony. Check the pony and the field. Pick out feet. Adjust the blanket, if one is worn, and replace it if it is very wet. Ride, if you have time. Feed and give hay.

◆ **Once a week:** Thoroughly check fencing. Pick up droppings.

Winter Tips

◆ Never make your pony stand around getting cold. If he is clipped, leave a blanket on until you are ready for a ride.
◆ If your pony is wet from sweating or from the rain when you come back from riding, you must not put a blanket on him until his coat is dry. Otherwise, he could easily catch a chill. He will dry quicker if you fit him with a string-vest anti-sweat sheet underneath another light blanket, or you could wipe the pony off with a handful of straw or dry towels.
◆ Avoid washing your pony (especially legs) too much in cold weather. Wait for mud to dry; then gently brush it off.
◆ You can feed a field-kept pony using a bucket hung on the gate. But, if his "friends" are around, this is sure to cause fights.

Cleaning Out

WHENEVER your pony is in a stable, he will need a thick, comfortable bed to keep him warm and to lie down on. It is true that ponies can doze standing up, but, to have a good rest, they must lie down or stretch out flat. If the bed is too thin, a pony won't like lying down. If he does lie down on it, he may risk getting bumps and scrapes.

STABLES must be cleaned out every day. It is a job many pony owners dislike. But, with daily practice, you will soon find it takes only a matter of minutes. It's not half as dirty and smelly as you might think.

A messy job, but it must be done...

1. Equip yourself with the right tools — a large wheelbarrow, a stable fork, a shovel, and a broom. For shavings or paper, use a shavings fork. A pair of rubber gloves can be handy to pick up scattered droppings.

2. Take the pony out of the stable — either turn him out or tie him up safely out of the way. Put the water buckets outside, too, and bring in the wheelbarrow.

3. Use the fork, shovel, and gloves to dig out the piles of droppings and put them into the barrow.

4. Now fork any clean bedding into one pile, the slightly dirty stuff into another, and the very dirty straight into the barrow.

5. Sweep the floor and corners clean, and empty the barrow onto the manure pile.

6. Fork the remaining piles back into the center. Add fresh bedding around the sides, shaking it out well. Make thick banks around the walls.

7. Once a week, leave the floor bare for a while. Disinfect it, and allow it to dry.

WITH shavings and paper, it is easier and more economical to pick up the droppings and wet parts daily and add some fresh bedding. Then do a thorough clean-out every one or two weeks.

"Deep litter" is a way of managing a bed where only the droppings are removed, and new bedding is piled on top. The whole bed is cleared only every few months. This sounds great, but it can lead to foot problems, such as thrush, unless great care is taken. Ventilation must be good, or the air in the stable becomes stale and smelly.

& Bedding

THERE are several different types of bedding from which to choose, each with its pros and cons. The most common are listed in the table *(below)*. There are other kinds of pre-packaged bedding, such as chopped hemp and dust-extracted straw. These are good for ponies that get a cough from a straw bed.

Although shavings and paper cost more than straw, there is a lot in each bale. With care, you might only need to use one or two bales a week. You could easily go through five or six straw bales in the same amount of time.

BEDDING	THE PROS	THE CONS
STRAW	Cheapest. Warm. Drains well. Easy to dispose of (rots well for garden fertilizer). Wheat straw is best. Oat or barley straw is more likely to be eaten!	Some ponies are allergic to the dust and spores in straw, which cause coughing. Needs to be stored under cover. Results in a lot of manure.
WOOD SHAVINGS	Better for dust-sensitive ponies. Easy to clean out. Comes in plastic-wrapped bales, so can be stored outside and brought in as needed.	Expensive. Takes a long time to rot, so could be hard to dispose of. Heavy to handle.
SHREDDED PAPER	Not as pricey as shavings. Warm. Rots faster than shavings but not as well as straw. Drains well. Dust-free. Can be stored outside and brought in as needed.	Blows everywhere in the wind!

Tips

Whatever bedding you use, put down plenty and spread it evenly. You should be able to stick the fork in and not be able to touch the floor.

The banks around the sides keep out drafts, protect against knocks if your pony should lie up against the wall, and help prevent him from getting "cast" — that is, lying down and finding he is wedged in and cannot get up again.

A manure pile attracts flies, so it should be well away from the stables. Try to keep it tidy, or it will soon be spreading in every direction.

Some ponies think their straw bed is there to be eaten. If you want to control nibbling, the only certain way is to change to a less tasty material.

FEEDING a pony correctly is one of the most important things an owner needs to learn. It is an important subject, but not quite as complicated as it seems as long as you stick to a few basic rules.

The first thing to remember is that every pony is different and has his own feeding needs, so you must find out what is best for your pony. Never just assume he will be fine eating what the next pony is eating.

The other point to bear in mind is that ponies' insides are quite different from those of other animals, such as ourselves. Ponies have amazingly intricate and delicate digestive systems that are easily upset, leading to problems like colic (a stomachache) that can be very serious. Lots of difficulties can come from being careless about feeding. So learn and stick to the *"Golden Rules of Feeding,"* and you will not go wrong.

Feeding:

1 Little and often

Nature designed horses and ponies to eat grass, taking in a little food at a time, almost all day long. They have small stomachs (about the size of a football) that cannot cope with big meals. A large quantity of food cannot be digested properly and could easily cause a blockage. Therefore, make sure that hay or grass is always available. Split concentrated feeds into several small meals a day. *Do not give more than 2 pounds (1 kilogram) of feed in one serving to a small pony or 3 pounds (1.5 kg) to a larger pony.*

2 Feed at regular times

Ponies like routine — and so do their stomachs! Stick to frequent, regular mealtimes that your pony will look forward to. Try not to dish up a large amount in one meal followed by a long period with no food at all.

4 Plenty of fiber

Fiber is roughage or bulk forage — food like grass, hay, or chaff. A horse's digestive system is designed to live on it. Without plenty of fiber trickling through, a pony's system cannot work properly. So, give him plenty of hay and high-fiber feeds like chaff and sugar beets, especially if your pony is stabled a lot.

3 Water supply

A pony will drink up to 10 gallons (36 liters) of water a day. He needs water to digest his food. But, remember, his stomach is small — so have water on hand all the time. Make sure he has had the chance to drink before a meal. Otherwise, he might chug water down and wash food away before it has been digested; or the water could make dry food swell painfully in the digestive system, which could cause a blockage.

5 Beware sudden changes

Ponies' insides are full of tiny microbes that break down and digest food. There is a unique microbe for every kind of food. That is why any alterations in the amount or kind of food you give have to be made gradually to give the digestive system time to adjust.

6 Feed the best quality

Do not buy cheap, poor-quality feed or keep foodstuffs for too long, or in damp or dusty conditions. Ponies cannot thrive on bad or musty food. It can actually make them ill. Feed the best you can afford, and store it properly in airtight, vermin-proof containers.

Golden Rules

7 Keep all your utensils clean

Would you like eating lunch off a plate no one had washed since yesterday's supper? Then don't expect your pony to enjoy his meal and stay healthy if he has to eat out of a grimy, grubby feed bucket. Cleaning food containers every day takes only a few minutes.

8 Wait at least an hour before exercise

The horse's ancestors needed to gallop away from predators at full speed, so they developed large lungs and small stomachs. A full stomach can make it hard for a pony to breathe easily because the stomach is just behind the lungs. Would you be comfortable exercising right after dinner?

9 Feed something succulent

Juicy grass is a pony's favorite food and the best thing for him (as long as he doesn't overdo it). But ponies appreciate succulent extras added to their feed. Apples, carrots, root vegetables, and sugar beet shreds are all enjoyed by ponies, especially those that don't get out into the field very often.

10 Feed as an individual

This is back where we started — learning that every pony has his own requirements when it comes to planning the amount and type of food he eats. His size, build, age, workload, character, the weather, and how he is kept are among the things you must consider.

NO WAY BACK!

Part of a pony's problem with feeding is that he cannot regurgitate, so, once he has swallowed a mouthful, it's in — for better or worse. The food then has to travel through over 98.5 feet (30 m) of intestines, taking up to three days, before it is passed. So, you can imagine — if he takes in something harmful — a lot of damage can be done.

KNOWING how to feed is only part of the feeding game. Now you need to study *what* your pony needs to eat if you want to keep him healthy and able to be his best. In just the same way that we are all supposed to eat a balanced, nutritious diet to keep healthy, ponies also need to get the right kind of food that contains a balance of all the important nutrients.

Feeding:

A PONY NEEDS . . .

CARBOHYDRATES: To provide energy to stay alive and do extra work, like being ridden.

PROTEIN: To build up cells and bones, and to help with healing, growth, and repair after illness or injury.

FIBER: To keep digestion working properly.

FATS: To keep warm and provide extra energy if needed.

VITAMINS AND MINERALS: To keep the body healthy and strong.

Different kinds of food contain different levels of nutrients, so it is not good to feed him just anything and hope for the best. For example, you might find you are feeding a high-carbohydrate diet that makes him so full of energy you have trouble staying on him.

Types of fiber

IN the wild, grass provides a pony with all the nutrients he needs. When one area has been grazed down, the herd moves on to a fresh, juicier place. But farms today are fenced into small fields. Although a well-managed pasture will provide enough nourishment in spring and summer, by autumn, it is not good for much. People have to replace that nourishment by providing grass in a dried form — hay. Grass and hay are the main sources of the bulk and fiber essential to a horse or pony's diet.

Grass
The best and most natural food for your pony. Good-quality grass will provide a complete, balanced diet during the spring and summer. When grass is poor — by autumn, in winter, during a very dry summer, or if the field is overgrazed — hay must be fed.

The two parts to a pony's diet

BESIDES water, a pony's diet is made up of either just one kind of food — bulk foods, such as grass and hay; or two kinds of food — bulk foods plus concentrated foods, such as pellets, mixes, or grains (oats or barley). A pony cannot survive without bulk fiber in his diet. He can live without concentrates, although they provide very useful extra energy that he needs for work and warmth.

Hay
This is grass cut and dried in early summer. It is stored to feed to horses in winter or when they are stabled. Feed only hay that is crisp, sweet-smelling, and contains a good mixture of nutritious grasses. Poor hay that is dusty, moldy, yellow, or full of weeds is bad for ponies. There are two types of hay — seed hay that has been grown specially, and meadow hay that is softer and finer and has been cut off the ordinary pasture. Hay can be fed from a rack or from a haynet. If you use a net, tie it high so, when it hangs empty, there is no risk of a pony's foot getting caught.

Fiber

Chaff
Usually straw, or a mix of hay and straw, that has been chopped up and is often covered with molasses. You can also buy alfalfa chaff that is a very nutritious clover-like plant, high in calcium. Chaff is a good way of adding fiber to the diet.

If you use a haynet, always tie it high up in the stable.

Haylage
Hay that has been treated and sealed into bags when it is half-dry. It is totally dust-free, so it is good for ponies sensitive to dust and spores in ordinary hay. It is a good alternative to hay, but it is very rich, so it must be fed sparingly.

TIP

SUCCULENT foods, like apples, carrots, root crops, and sugar beets, also have a high fiber content. Always chop them lengthways to avoid the risk of the pony choking. Do not overfeed, or you may give your pony diarrhea.

1

2

BULK forage by itself can keep a pony going along fine, but it doesn't contain much energy. In winter, most of the energy it does have is used just keeping the pony warm. Whenever a pony is being ridden regularly or the weather is harsh, he will probably need extra meals of concentrate or "hard feed."

Some ponies, especially cob or draft types, need very little or no concentrate feed because they are such "easy-keepers" — that is, they thrive on relatively little feed. Other ponies tend to lose weight or feel the cold unless they are given plenty of concentrates in addition to their hay and grass.

Whatever concentrates are given, the balance of nutrients in them must be just right. So it is important to know something about the different types of foodstuffs, particularly if you plan to mix several kinds. Compound feeds, such as pellets or coarse mixes, are excellent. The manufacturer has done all of the thinking for you, taking the worry and effort out of making up a diet for your pony. It also means that you do not have to buy various bags of different feeds that always seem to run out at different times!

Feeding:

Choices on the Menu...

Pellets/cubes

◆ A balanced mixture of traditional foodstuffs, crushed and pressed into pellets.

◆ Far and away the best (and most economical) hard feed for almost all riding ponies and horses. Together with water and hay/grass, they contain all the nutrition your pony needs.

◆ **Watch out!** There is no need to add anything else to a diet of pellets except chaff and apples/carrots, or you will upset the formula.

◆ Buy the right type of pellets, as there are different kinds. There are certain pellets for ponies doing little work and certain pellets for competition horses, brood mares, and youngsters.

Q & A

QUESTION: Does my pony need a vitamin or mineral supplement?

ANSWER: If he's in good health and getting a balanced diet, the answer is most probably "no." Growing or hard-working ponies might need supplements. Your vet can advise a supplement to help with special problems like cracked feet.

Varieties of hard feed
(from left):
1 Pellets
2 Coarse mix
3 Rolled oats
4 Flaked barley
5 Flaked corn

Hard Feeds

Choices on the Menu...

Choices on the Menu...

Coarse mix

◆ A ready-formulated mix like pellets, but bought in muesli form.

◆ Great for pony owners, for the same reasons as pellets.

◆ **Watch out!** *(See Pellets on previous page).*

Oats

◆ Bought crushed, rolled, or bruised so they are easily digested.

◆ For ponies doing a lot of work.

◆ **Watch out!** Guaranteed to wake up the doziest pony. Oats must be fed with a calcium-rich food to maintain the right balance of two important minerals — calcium and phosphorus.

Barley

◆ Bought flaked, micronized, or extruded (forms of cooking). Whole barley can be boiled into a mash.

◆ Gives energy to ponies in regular work. Good for putting on weight and for warmth.

◆ **Watch out!** Can heat up some ponies. Should not make up more than a third of the total feeding.

Flaked corn

◆ Used for hard-working ponies, in small amounts.

◆ **Watch out!** High in energy and also phosphorus. Feed sparingly.

Broad bran

◆ Traditionally, given as a mash for resting, sick, or old horses. When prepared in this way, it works as a laxative.

◆ **Watch out!** Besides being expensive, it can cause calcium deficiency. Adding chaff to the feed is a better source of fiber.

Dried sugar beets

◆ Come as shreds or pellets, with added molasses.

◆ Good for adding fiber to hard feeds. High in energy and calcium. Tasty.

◆ **Watch out!** Must be soaked in water for at least twelve hours before feeding. Do not keep soaked beets for more than forty-eight hours because the mixture ferments. Don't confuse beet pellets with similar-looking, ordinary pony pellets.

Minerals, Vitamins

The only essential mineral you will need to add to your pony's diet is a teaspoonful of salt. Add to the feed daily or put a salt lick on the stable wall.

HALF the secret of feeding is knowing how much to give. It takes experience to judge whether your pony is looking too heavy and needs less food, too thin and needs more, or is in exactly the right condition. As a rough guide, if you can feel his ribs when you press your fingers on his sides, he is about right. If his ribs can be seen, he is too thin. If you can't feel a hint of ribs, he's too heavy. Being heavy isn't a healthy sign. A heavy pony is at risk for serious diseases, such as laminitis *(see page 45)*.

In summer, few ponies need extra food on top of the grass in the field. In fact, many do so well on spring and summer grass that they may need their grazing limited by being brought in for part of the day. Or the pasture may have to be chained off to stop the ponies from getting overweight.

If dry weather burns the grass, it may be necessary to feed some hay, but only hard-working ponies are likely to need any concentrated feed in summer. In winter, keep a close eye on your pony's condition, and decide whether he needs hard feed on top of his hay to maintain his weight and energy for the work he does. Study the information on pages 20-21 to plan a personal diet for your pony.

Feeding:

Draft pony

13hh
Bodyweight: 550 pounds (250 kg)
Lives: Out all year.
Work: Daily ride in summer, weekends only in winter.
Daily diet: Summer — grass only. Winter — 13 pounds (6 kg) hay, 2-3.5 pounds (1-1.5kg) pellets or low energy mix, plus a handful of chaff and carrots.

Diets

Competition pony

14.2hh
Bodyweight: 880 pounds (400 kg)
Lives: Out in summer, in at nights in winter. Or in at nights all year.
Work: Ridden every day in summer, including trail rides, schooling, jumping, regular shows. Daily work throughout winter, including shows and lessons.
Daily diet: Summer — grass with 6.5 pounds (3 kg) hay at night if brought in, 6.5-9 pounds (3-4 kg) pellets, plus chaff and carrots. Winter — 11-15.5 pounds (5-7 kg) hay, 9-11 pounds (4-5 kg) pellets or mix, plus chaff and carrots. Or, 5.5-6.5 pounds (2.5-3 kg) pellets/mix, 11 pounds (5 kg) barley or oats, 2 pounds (1 kg) sugar beets, plus a handful of chaff.

Draft-cross pony

14hh
Bodyweight: 770 pounds (350 kg)
Lives: Out in summer, in at nights in winter.
Work: Daily rides, some shows. In winter, two or three weekday rides plus occasional lesson/rally.
Daily diet: Summer — grass, plus 4.5-5.5 pounds (2-2.5 kg) pellets or low-energy mix, only if necessary. Winter — 13-15 pounds (6-7 kg) hay, 5.5-7.5 pounds (2.5-3.5 kg) pellets or low-energy mix, plus a handful of chaff and carrots.

1. Basic amount

The basic amount of food a pony needs each day is determined according to his body weight. He will require approximately 2 pounds (1 kg) of food a day per 1,100 pounds (500 kg) of bodyweight.

Horses and ponies are never weighed on a scale. Their weight is determined by a mathematical formula involving estimates of their height and the diameters of their chest, barrel, and rump.

Feeding:

2. How much bulk/fiber and concentrate?

How much of this total should be made up of hay/grass and how much of hard feed? Basically, the more work a pony is doing, the greater proportion can be made up of hard feed *(see panel, below)*. But never give less than 50 percent of the total as bulk.

Bulk vs. Concentrate

	grass/hay	*concentrate*
No work or occasional/ weekend rides	100%	none, unless weather poor or grass scarce
Regular rides/lessons	70-80%	20-30%
Daily long or fast rides/ lessons/shows	60%	40%

Feed vs. Lifestyle

General riding	Non-heating pellets or low-energy coarse mix, perhaps with a handful of chaff and apples/carrots added.
Ponies with special needs	Hard-working — performance mix/pellets, or make up a ration including some barley/oats and sugar beets.
	Lose weight easily or feel the cold — try including barley and sugar beets.
	Old ponies — include sugar beets, boiled barley, and alfalfa chaff.

3. What sort of concentrate?

Choose the feed that suits your pony and his lifestyle to make up this part of the ration *(see panel, bottom left)*.

DO not just guess at feed weights. Check the weight of a scoopful of each kind of feed you are using *(opposite)*. Weigh hay by hooking a haynet to spring-scales that you can buy cheaply from any feed merchant or tack shop.

Quantities

4. When might my pony need less feed?

Remember, you have to be flexible about feeding. Use your common sense concerning your pony's condition. If any of the points below apply, he may not need quite as much food as the total you have calculated.

◆ In the spring and summer, especially when the grass starts growing.

◆ If he is a very easy-keeper or prone to laminitis. Many ponies get fat easily and do well on relatively little food.

◆ If he is getting too lively to ride or handle, he may be getting too much or the wrong sort of food. Reduce the amount of concentrate he is getting and increase the hay/grass.

◆ If he has a live-wire temperament, he may need very little hard feed. Feed only low-energy pellets or a high-fiber mix.

5. When should I increase the amount I feed my pony?

The quantity you feed may need to be increased:

◆ If the pony is not doing well on what he is getting and if he looks thin or has no energy. Look at his teeth, and check if he needs worming. Increase his hay and time in the field, then his hard feed.

◆ Any time when the grass is poor or scarce.

◆ During bad weather, particularly if he lives out or is clipped.

◆ When your pony is working hard, such as during school holidays.

◆ For in-foal mares, youngsters, and older ponies that don't process their food efficiently. These animals have special needs. Discuss with your vet.

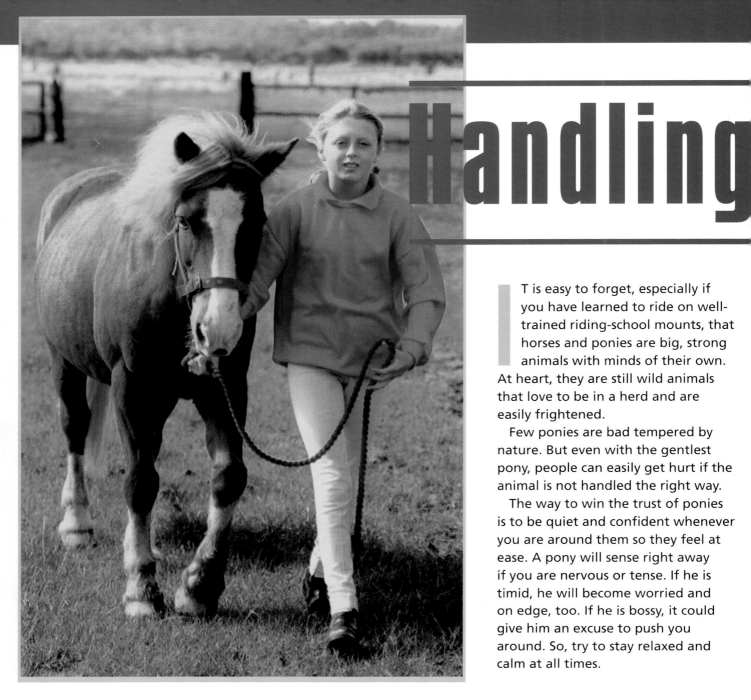

Handling

T is easy to forget, especially if you have learned to ride on well-trained riding-school mounts, that horses and ponies are big, strong animals with minds of their own. At heart, they are still wild animals that love to be in a herd and are easily frightened.

Few ponies are bad tempered by nature. But even with the gentlest pony, people can easily get hurt if the animal is not handled the right way.

The way to win the trust of ponies is to be quiet and confident whenever you are around them so they feel at ease. A pony will sense right away if you are nervous or tense. If he is timid, he will become worried and on edge, too. If he is bossy, it could give him an excuse to push you around. So, try to stay relaxed and calm at all times.

LEADING A PONY SAFELY

LEADING is one of the most basic handling and safety skills you need to learn because it is easy to get stepped on, to get taken for a walk by the pony, or even to lose him altogether. Ponies are a lot stronger than people, so the trick is not to let them realize this!

◆ Although a pony should get used to being led from either side, it is most common to lead from his left (near) side. If you ever have to lead a pony on the road, always place yourself between him and the oncoming traffic, and use a bridle rather than a halter.

◆ Hold the lead rope about 10 inches (25 centimeters) away from the pony's chin with your right hand (left hand if leading from the right-hand side). If he is trotting, allow a little more rope to give more freedom for his head. Hold the rest of the rope in your other hand, keeping it off the ground.

◆ Walk right alongside the pony's head. Do not drag him along behind you or let him charge off in front.

◆ Do not hold onto the rope too tightly or too close to his head. Ponies hate feeling pressure or restriction on their heads and might panic.

◆ Never wrap the lead rope around your hand or wrist. If the pony takes fright, you could be dragged along.

◆ If you want to turn the pony's body for a vet or in the show ring, always turn him away from you. This avoids getting your toes squashed and gives a clear view of his movement.

◆ If you are leading a tacked-up pony, make sure the stirrup irons are run up, not dangling. Take the reins over the pony's head. If he wears a running martingale, unbuckle the reins and unthread it. Then tie it in a loose knot, and hold the reins over his head.

Hints

ALWAYS speak to a pony when you approach or handle him so he knows where you are. Never move suddenly or make loud, unexpected noises. Ponies cannot see behind them or very well in front of them, so walk steadily up to the pony's shoulder to let him see you, and stroke him firmly on the neck. Ponies love to be touched and scratched, as it is their own way of greeting each other. If you want to offer a snack, make this an occasional treat rather than something your pony demands every time you appear. Hold your hand out flat so no fingers are mistaken for juicy pieces of carrot.

Speaking to your pony can help him understand what you want him to do. Make commands definite, such as, "over" or "walk on." Praise him in a kind, soft voice. If he needs to be disciplined, make it a stern, sharp "no!" Both should come right away, not when he has forgotten what he did right or wrong. Always be fair and consistent in the way you treat and handle ponies so they know what is right and wrong behavior.

Hold your hand out flat when feeding a pony. This hand position (left) is incorrect.

BEING tied up for grooming, cleaning out, or shoeing is one of the first things a young pony learns. But there is always a danger that something might startle even the quietest pony when he is tied up, which is when accidents can happen.

- Never leave a pony tied up alone.
- Leave plenty of space in between ponies tied up next to each other, especially if they are eating.
- Do not make the rope so short that your pony can hardly move his head, or so long that he could put a foot over it and get tangled up.
- Never tie up using your reins — one tug and you have a broken bridle. Always put a halter on over your bridle and use the proper lead rope.
- Never tie your pony to a movable object, such as an open gate.
- Always attach your pony to something easily breakable in case disaster strikes and he needs to move away. Try a loop of string tied to a fixed post or rail.
- Use a secure knot that your pony cannot undo, but you can — in a hurry if need be. Practice your quick-release knot and use it.

Tying a quick-release knot

1. **Push a loop of lead rope through your string. Twist the loop several times.**
2. **Make another loop of the free end of the rope and push it through the twisted loop.**
3. **To tighten, pull on the end of the rope attached to the halter.**
4. **The knot can be quickly and completely released by pulling on the free end of the rope.**

Handling

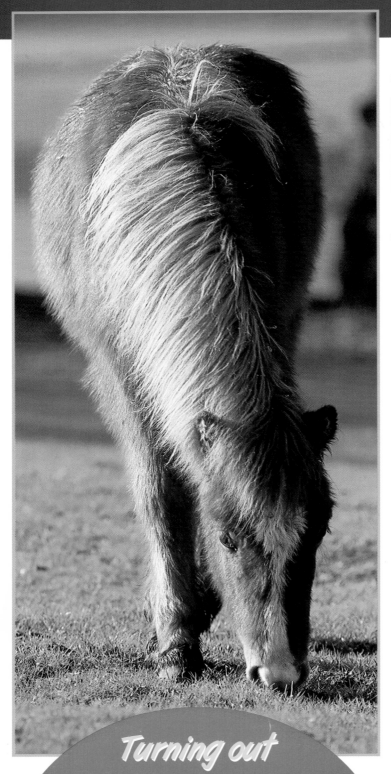

MOST ponies live outdoors for most of the year or are at least turned out often. So it is necessary to know how to move around among loose ponies, how to turn a pony out, and how to catch a pony.

Ponies kept out together soon start to behave like a mini-herd. Anything out of the ordinary, such as a new arrival, nearby activity, or stormy weather, can make them excited or wary.

You will notice that there are bossy characters and shy ones. Sometimes you may see ponies rearing up or kicking in the field. They rarely mean to hurt each other at these times.

Usually, bad-tempered faces, laid-back ears, and lifted heels are a warning to other ponies to "watch out." But this natural behavior means that humans need to watch out, too, when visiting a field full of ponies. You don't want to be on the end of a kick.

Turning out

SWINGING open the gate and letting a pony go with a slap on the bottom is asking for trouble. Teach your pony to be well mannered and to stay safe by:

◆ Always opening the gate wide enough to pass through, but keeping hold of it as you go.

◆ Leading the pony through and shutting the gate behind you — otherwise, the rest of the field occupants could disappear!

◆ Walking a little way in and turning your pony around to face the gate. Make him stand quietly for a few moments before carefully slipping his halter off.

◆ Never releasing him facing into the field — he could soon be over the horizon with you still attached!

Awkward customers...

Some ponies are not that easy to get your hands on. Maybe the spring grass is too tasty, or they don't like the idea of work. Are there problems that you can correct? Make sure your pony always associates being caught with pleasant experiences. Here are some tips:

◆ Never grab at your pony or lose your temper. Do not try cornering or chasing him. He's quicker than you, and you will be worn out long before he is.

Hints

Catching a pony

◆ **Walk into the field steadily and confidently,** speaking so the ponies have time to see and hear you. Hold the halter neatly by your side.

◆ **By all means, have a treat in your pocket to reward your pony for being caught. But it is a bad idea to take a bucket into a field full of ponies. Before you know it, you will be in the middle of a riot!**

◆ **Approach at an angle to your pony's shoulder. With a friendly word and pat on the neck, slip the lead rope around his neck. Put the halter around his nose, fix the headstrap securely, and walk him quietly toward the gate.**

◆ **Even if your pony is standing by the gate, never lean over and put the halter on over the gate. Do not take such risks with ponies.**

◆ **Be patient, and give yourself plenty of time. Be prepared to make several visits just to catch him, feed him, and fuss over him until he starts to change his mind about being caught.**

◆ **When you do get hold of him, always reward him. Never scold him, or he definitely won't come next time.**

◆ **Persistent offenders can be turned out in a well-fitting leather halter with a short length — about 10 inches (25 cm) — of rope attached.**

◆ **Tactics for catching persistent offenders include fencing off a small corner of the field to lure your pony into, walking around him in ever-decreasing circles, walking after him until he gives up, or sitting down and waiting for his curiosity to overcome his reluctance.**

Grooming:

GROOMING a pony obviously makes him look more beautiful. But a much more important reason for grooming is to keep his skin and coat healthy and clean. Different ponies will have different grooming routines according to what kind of lifestyle they lead.

Ponies who are stabled a lot need a thorough grooming every day to clean their skin and keep their coats in top condition. They need a quick brush-over before exercise.

By putting effort into your brushing, you can even improve the pony's circulation and muscle tone. If your pony lives outside, do not go to an extreme with your grooming. He needs to keep plenty of grease and oil in his coat for warmth and waterproofing, especially during winter. Field-kept ponies still need to be brushed over before a ride, though, and will appreciate being kept comfortable and tidy.

Grooming is a perfect way to get to know a pony well. Although some ponies are particularly ticklish, most love being groomed. It probably feels like a relaxing massage to them. It's also a perfect chance for you to look your pony over for minor cuts, lumps, and injuries — and to keep an eye on his general condition.

for Health

EVEN if you don't own your own pony, collecting the gear of a grooming kit means you will be better prepared to help out at the stables. You will need:

1. **Dandy brush:** A large brush with long, stiff bristles for removing mud, dirt, and dried sweat. Too hard to use on the head, mane, or tail.
2. **Body brush:** A softer brush with shorter, denser bristles that cleans deep down into the coat.
3. **Hoof pick:** Removes bedding, mud, and stones.
4. **Hoof oil:** Brushed onto the feet for beauty.
5. **Rubber or plastic curry comb:** Gets dry mud off and removes loose hair during springtime molting.

6. **Metal curry comb:** Never use on the pony's body. Scrape it across the body brush to remove the hairs, dust, and scurf (flaky scales) collected there.
7. **Water brush:** Like a dandy brush with shorter, softer bristles. For scrubbing hooves and wetting the mane and top of the tail so they lie flat.
8. **Sponges:** For bathing and freshening up the eyes, nostrils, or dock (solid part of the tail).
9. **Stable rubber:** A cloth used to give an extra polish to the coat or to dry damp areas.
10. **Mane comb:** For final combing through of the mane and then braiding.

The Gear

Grooming:

After a day in the field

TIP

CAUTION: Mud, grass, or stable stains need to be *wiped* off. Use a brush only when your pony's coat is dry. Brushing wet hair will not remove dirt, and it will scratch and chafe the skin.

If your pony is wet from the rain and you want to ride, scrape off as much wet as you can using a sweat scraper, then rub the saddle area with a towel. Do not put the saddle on until the coat has had a chance to dry properly.

◆ Use the hoof pick twice daily to clear mud and stones from the feet.

◆ Carefully sponge the eyes, nose, and dock, using separate sponges for each.

When cleaning eyes, wipe from back to front so dirt is not spread across the eye.

◆ If you are going for a ride, freshen up your pony by using the rubber curry comb to get off most of the mud.

◆ Now take the dandy brush and use it back-and-forth across the body, especially over the areas where the tack goes. Dirt left on there can cause sores. Around the head, it is best to use your fingers to pick off dry mud. Then use the softer body brush.

◆ Use the body brush over the entire body once in a while, but not every day. Take out tangles from the mane and tail with your fingers. Then finish the job with the body brush.

Routines

TIP

SOME ponies will not pick their feet up for grooming immediately when you ask. If this happens, stay close to the leg and lean slightly into the pony's side. Nudge him with your shoulder or elbow until he shifts his weight and gives you the chance to lift his foot. Do not lift a foot up too high because this is very uncomfortable for the pony.

Picking out feet

TO pick up and clean out the feet, take your hoof pick and stand alongside the pony's shoulder, facing his tail. Stroke his shoulder firmly, then run your hand down the back of the leg. When you reach the fetlock, gently tug the hair and say "up."

Hold the front of the hoof with your fingers. With the hoof pick in your outside hand, scrape from the heel toward the toe. Scraping in this direction avoids hurting the sensitive frog (*V*-shaped part of the sole).

For the hind legs, stand close alongside the pony's quarters. Pet him firmly, and talk to him. Run your hand down the inside of the leg past the hock to the fetlock. Hold the fetlock in the back, and ask the pony to lift it like before. Again, hold the foot with your fingers so the pony does not lean on you.

When you have finished cleaning the foot, don't just drop it. Put it down fully, or you could accidentally get kicked as the pony waves his foot around.

Grooming

I F the pony you ride spends a lot of time in the stable, you can give him a complete grooming fairly often. It is best to groom thoroughly after a ride because this is when his skin will be warm. Just before a show is another time you might want to give your pony a complete grooming. Field-kept ponies will also benefit from having a complete grooming once in a while.

Complete routine

◆ Tie up your pony and pick out each foot. (See Picking out feet, page 29).

◆ Brush off any dry dirt and sweat marks with the dandy brush or rubber curry comb. Start at the top of the neck and work down the body and legs.

◆ Tease out the mane with your fingers. Then work through it with the body brush. Now do the same with the tail.

◆ Starting near the head, groom the body with the body brush. Use firm, circular strokes, putting all your weight behind each one and always brushing in the direction of the hair. Every few strokes, scrape the brush across the metal curry comb to clean it. Clean the curry comb by tapping it on the floor.

◆ Undo the halter. If the door to the barn is shut, remove the halter so you can gently brush the head with the body brush. If you are outside, keep holding the rope around the pony's neck. Put the halter back on when you finish.

◆ Sponge the eyes, nose, and dock.

◆ You can "lay" the mane, using a damp water brush, to keep it flat.

ALWAYS use a brush in the hand nearest the pony's head. So, when grooming the near (left) side, use your left hand; and, on the off (right) side, use your right hand.

◆ Use the water brush to wash any mud off the feet. When the feet are dry, brush on some hoof oil for a finishing touch.

◆ Wipe the entire body with a slightly damp stable rubber for a final glossing and dusting.

& Bathing

ON hot summer days or for that special occasion when your pony needs to be extra beautiful, a bath is beneficial. It will do his coat good, and it will keep flies away. You can wash the tail more often in any kind of weather, even winter. Avoid giving full baths in winter because the pony could catch a chill.

Bath time tips

◆ Many ponies dislike water or may not be used to being bathed. Make sure a helper is available to hold the pony while you carefully introduce him to water.

◆ Never slosh the water around unnecessarily. Be especially careful if you are using a hose because this can frighten a pony.

◆ Use lukewarm water, except on hot days. Ponies don't like cold showers any more than you do!

◆ Always use a formulated horse shampoo. Many ponies have very sensitive skin.

◆ Dampen the coat and mane with the sponge or hose, then apply the shampoo (but not too much). Rub it in gently. Now rinse it off well, changing the water as you need to or using the hose.

◆ Use the sweat scraper to wipe off excess water.

The hard edge is for the body, and the flexible edge is for the legs.

◆ Take care not to get shampoo in your pony's eyes.

◆ When washing the tail, stand slightly to one side. Soak it, then apply a little shampoo and rub it in. Rinse it out thoroughly, squeeze out most of the water, and swing the tail around gently to help it dry.

◆ Use a towel to dry the heels well.

◆ Walk the pony around until he is dry, then go over him with the body brush. If there is a chill in the air, a sweat blanket with a light cotton sheet on top will help him dry without getting cold.

◆ Remember, if you let your pony loose in the field with a damp coat, he is sure to roll in the dust.

Trimming

THERE are several places on a pony you can use scissors in order to make him look better. On the whole, it is best not to get carried away with the trimming on a field-kept pony, especially in winter. He grows all that hair for a very good reason. But a bit of trimming will tidy him up and do no harm.

WHISKERS: Kind, caring owners never trim off a pony's whiskers. He uses them all the time to feel and judge the distance between his nose and the ground. However, show ponies are often trimmed, and it does them no harm.

CHIN: Snip off the long hairs that grow under the chin and jaw-line.

EARS: Carefully trim hair from the outside edges of the ears, but not the inside. That fuzz protects the delicate inside of the ear. Show ponies, however, are clipped on the inside of the ear, and it does them no harm.

POLL: People like to cut a "bridle-path" out of the mane behind the ears so the bridle head-piece can sit easier there.

HEELS: It is not a good idea to trim hair from the heels of an outdoor pony in winter, as the long hair generally helps drain rainwater away. An exception is in areas of clay soil that clogs and sticks around the fetlocks. Use a mane comb to lift the hair the opposite way and cut it upward. Again, show ponies are often trimmed, and it does them no harm.

Braiding the tail

BRAIDING looks beautiful on a pony with a full tail. Take a few hairs from each side at the top of the tail and fasten them with thread. Use this as your center strand. Take a few more hairs from each side (as your side strands) and start to braid. Continue down the tail, taking more hairs from the sides and keeping the braid tight and flat in the middle of the tail. When you reach the end of the tailbone, keep braiding to the end of the long hairs. Secure this with thread or a rubber band, loop it up to the bottom of the braid, and stitch it so it lies flat.

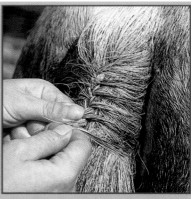

"Pulling" the mane & tail

MANES and tails can be tidied up by thinning them out. This is called "pulling." It is best not to pull the tail of any pony that spends time in the field because the thickness of the tail protects him from the cold wind and rain. All ponies can have their manes pulled, but remember not to take too much if your pony lives outdoors because his thick mane keeps his neck warm. Save pulling for a mild day, after you have come back from a ride and when the skin will be warm and the pores open. Using a proper pulling comb, take a few hairs from underneath the mane. Wrap them around the comb and pull sharply. Only do a few at a time, or you will make your pony sore.

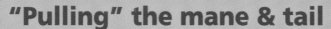

& Braiding

THERE'S nothing like a neat row of braids on a special occasion. Braiding is an art, and practice makes perfect. Keep trying, and you will soon be producing some really top knots!

How to braid a mane

1 Tie your pony up. It really helps to make tidy braids if your pony's mane is not too thick and long. Shorten and thin it by careful pulling *(see opposite)*. Then, thoroughly brush the mane to one side. Dampen it with a water brush. Divide it into equal sections, one for each braid. Make the partings as neat as you can with no stray hairs. Fasten each bunch loosely with a rubber band.

2 Stand well above your pony on something safe, and take the first bunch. Divide it into three equal strands. Holding the hair slightly up and away from the crest, braid to the bottom by placing the right-hand strand over the center one, then the left over the center, and so on. Pull the braid tightly as you go along.

3 At the end, hold the braid firmly. Take the rubber band and wind it around several times. Hold on tightly or it will unravel. Tuck away any loose hairs neatly under the band.

4 Now, fold the braid in half, keeping the end underneath, then, in half again, to create a "bobble," or small ball. Take another rubber band and twist it tightly around the whole bobble several times to secure it to the crest.

5 Do each bunch, one by one, in this way until the entire mane is braided. Finish with the forelock to complete the picture.

THERE are no hard and fast rules about how many braids to do, but tradition says there should be an odd number down the neck plus one for the forelock.

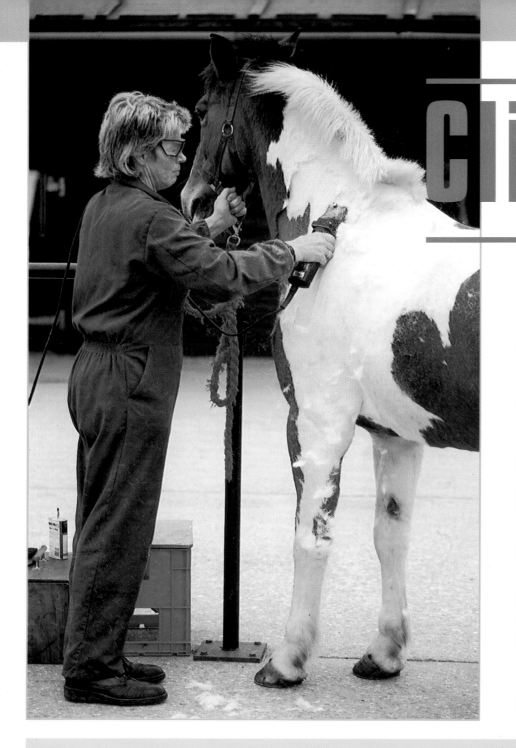

Clipping

TIP

Gently does it...

MOST ponies that are carefully introduced to clipping do not mind it.

However, it is a job for an expert. Ask your stable to recommend a professional.

A clip will probably be necessary every six to eight weeks. But don't clip immediately after winter or it will prohibit your pony's summer coat from coming through.

Why your pony might need a clip

BY the time autumn comes around, most ponies have begun to grow the thick, woolly coats designed to protect them against the cold, wet weather that is on the way. Without that fuzz, they would lose body warmth and weight very quickly. The trouble is that, while these winter woollies are great protection when a pony is out in the field, they also make him very hot when out for a ride on a mild day.

Sweating a lot is not good for a pony and will soon make him lose condition. Drying off a sweaty pony is a real chore. Dried-on sweat is hard to brush off.

By clipping away part of the winter coat, the pony can be kept comfortable while he is working. Regular groomings will also be easier.

But not every pony benefits from clipping. Whether or not you need to clip, and the style you choose, depend on how your pony lives and the work he does. There is no point clipping off your pony's natural warmth-layer only to pile on more blankets and give him more feed unnecessarily. Remember, a pony without his natural coat could get very cold, especially if he lives outside. Then, any hair taken off must be replaced by blankets *(see pages 36-39)*.

Types of clips

Neck and belly clip

For ponies ridden on weekends and holidays only. Can be used on a pony living outside, with a New Zealand blanket. If your pony is ridden only occasionally in winter, he is better off not being clipped.

Trace clip

Can be low, medium, or high, depending on how much is taken off. Suitable for ponies in regular work. Leaving the neck partially untrimmed is best for ponies that feel the cold.

Chaser clip

Suits ponies like the trace clip does.

Blanket clip

Hair is left on the back and quarters like a blanket. Best for hard-working ponies that are kept mainly stabled.

Hunter clip

Only the saddle patch and legs are left untrimmed. Suitable only for very hard-working ponies that don't spend much time in the field. A pony with this clip must be well blanketed if he is turned out.

Blankets:

DEPENDING on your pony's lifestyle, you may need to buy blankets to keep him warm in winter. Tough and hardy draft ponies grow incredibly thick coats that give them better weather protection than any blanket. If your pony is this type and is not clipped and he has good shelter in the field, there may be no need for him to wear a blanket. However, other types of ponies that live outside will appreciate wearing an outdoor blanket. They will certainly need one if they are clipped.

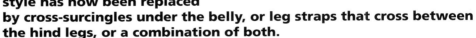

New Zealand blanket

THIS is the blanket that is worn outdoors. It is made of waterproof fabric that was traditionally thick canvas. Now, most modern blankets are made of lighter-weight, human-made materials.

New Zealands need to fit well to make sure they stay in place during rolling, bucking, and galloping. Old-fashioned blankets used to have a surcingle (belt) around the girth. This uncomfortable style has now been replaced by cross-surcingles under the belly, or leg straps that cross between the hind legs, or a combination of both.

A New Zealand should be wide enough to keep out the wind, and it should be big enough to give the pony freedom of movement without rubbing. But it should not be so loose and baggy that it lets in drafts or slips around. Remember, a canvas blanket will need re-waterproofing after every winter.

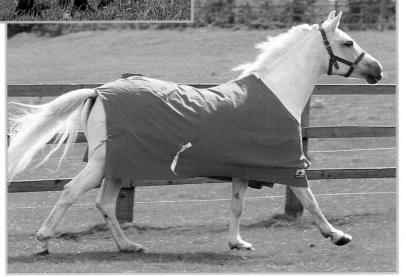

The blanket must fit well and not inhibit movement in case your pony decides to buck (top), gallop (left), or roll (above).

Types

THE other main blanket you may need is a stable blanket that is worn when your pony comes indoors. Even if your pony is unclipped, when he is stabled he cannot move around much and may get cold in chilly weather without a blanket.

Most modern stable blankets are made of synthetic materials, often quilted. They fasten using surcingles that cross under the belly. In the past, blankets were secured using a wide strap, called a roller, around the girth. But this could easily put pressure on the spine and was not very comfortable for the horse or pony.

In very cold weather or following a clip, you may need to add extra layers underneath a stable blanket. You can use either an under-blanket with its own fastenings, or what is known as a "house" blanket. If you use a house blanket, it will need to be kept in place using a roller over the top of all the layers. Fasten the roller firmly (not overtight). Use a thick pad over the pony's backbone if the roller is not the kind that is styled to stay clear of the spine.

Stable Blanket

Other types

SUMMER SHEET

THIS is usually a lightweight sheet made of a cotton mix. It is used in summer when traveling or for keeping the dust and flies off.

Some types are designed to help a sweaty pony dry quickly. These can also be used under a stable blanket to keep its lining clean.

SWEAT BLANKET

THE string-vest kind of blanket is often seen on show ponies or on winning race-horses. It works by trapping pockets of air that allow the horse to cool without getting cold. It can do this only if the air is trapped, so it must always be used with another blanket on top. In warm weather, this could be a cotton summer sheet. In colder weather, a woolen cooler or stable blanket would be suitable.

COOLER

A blanket, usually made of wool, used when traveling in winter.

EXERCISE SHEET

A USEFUL addition to any pony's wardrobe is an exercise sheet. Fasten it on your pony under the saddle. It will keep rain off him during a winter ride. That means your pony will arrive home dry, and you can place your pony's New Zealand or stable blanket immediately back on him.

Blankets:

BLANKETS range in size from about 4.5 feet (138 cm) long for a tiny pony to 6 feet (182 cm) long for a small horse. To get approximately the right size for your pony, measure from the point of the chest (between the forelegs) all the way along the body to the point of the buttock (below the tail). The blanket should be long enough to just cover the tail and the buttocks, and wide enough to go well below the belly and elbows. A well-fitted blanket sits neatly over the shoulders and follows the line of the back.

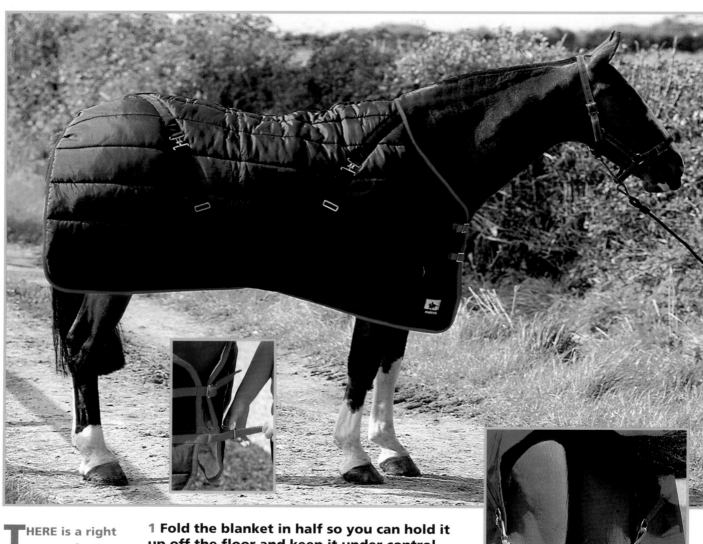

THERE is a right way and a wrong way to put on and take off blankets — both for safety's sake and the comfort of the pony.

1 **Fold the blanket in half so you can hold it up off the floor and keep it under control. You do not want it flapping around and alarming your pony.**
2 **Put it over the pony, well forward, still folded. Fasten the front straps** *(inset).*
3 **Fold it back, adjust it, and fasten the belly straps or hind-leg straps. Pull back slightly into place.**
4 **On a New Zealand blanket, cross the hind-leg straps over to keep the blanket in place and to keep it from rubbing the legs** *(right).*

Fitting

How to put a blanket on

TO put a house blanket on underneath a stable blanket (*above*), place it over the pony. Then fold the front corners up to the withers. Put the stable blanket on top and fasten. Now, fold back the *V* of the blanket and fasten it underneath the roller. Make sure the roller has no twists in it and is clear of the spine.

Taking it off ...

WHEN taking a blanket off, work in the opposite direction, from back to front. Undo the straps nearest the pony's back end first, then the belly, then the front. Either fold the blanket forward and slip it off from the side, or stand by the quarters and slip it off backward with the lie of the hair.

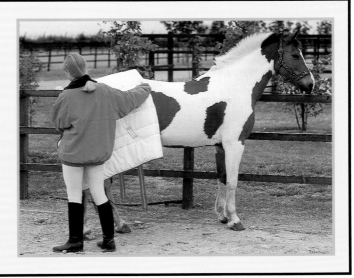

Shoeing

THROUGHOUT evolution, the horse has relied upon his feet to carry him swiftly out of danger. Like human fingernails, horses' hooves grow continually. In the past, wild horses constantly moved over rough ground, and so their feet wore naturally into shape. It is equally important to the modern, domesticated horse or pony to have healthy feet. But, from living in a stable or small field, their hooves grow long and cracked. If the hooves are not regularly trimmed, the horse or pony becomes uncomfortable and unbalanced.

Riding — especially on a very hard surface, like a road — wears down the hooves faster than they can grow. So most of these riding horses and ponies need to wear metal shoes to stop their feet from getting sore.

Trimming the feet and shoeing are the jobs of the farrier, an extremely skilled craftsperson who trains for many years before becoming qualified to shoe. Although a pony's foot might look hard and lifeless from the outside, beneath the outer horn or hoof wall are layers of super-sensitive tissues and nerves and the crucial bones that keep the horse or pony on his feet.

"No foot, no horse" is a true saying. Imagine trying to run and jump in uncomfortable shoes…

When to call the farrier

MOST ponies need the farrier every six to eight weeks. Even if the shoes are not loose or worn, do not wait much longer than this because the hooves will have grown too long for the shoes. If necessary, the farrier can trim the hooves back and replace the old shoes, saving you some cost — this is called "removes." Here are some signs that a pony needs the farrier:

- The shoes are thin and worn.
- The toes or heels are overgrowing the shoe, or the foot is starting to look long and flat.
- A shoe is loose or twisted or has been lost.
- The pony has started stumbling more than usual.

A well-shod foot

HERE are some things to look for in a well-shod foot:
- The shoe has been made to fit the foot — never the other way around.
- There is no daylight between the foot and shoe.
- The clenches (nails) are evenly spaced and level.
- The frog is still in contact with the ground — this is the pony's anti-slip device.
- The heels of the shoe are not too long.
- The foot has been evenly trimmed at both the toe and heel.

Hot shoe for a better fit

IT is very important that your pony's shoes fit him, as he will not be able to move comfortably if they do not. Most farriers shoe "hot" *(below)* because this tends to give the best fit. It is possible to shoe "cold," without heating the shoe, but fewer adjustments can be made to a cold shoe. Although a good fit is still possible, as a rule, hot shoeing is better.

From left: *The old shoe is taken off with a buffer and hammer. Overgrown hoof wall is trimmed with a drawing knife. The new shoe is heated in a forge and hammered into shape. The new shoe is put in place with nails hammered through the dead wall of the foot.*

Step-by-step . . .

1 First, your farrier will look at each foot to see how the old shoes have worn. He or she then uses a buffer and hammer to cut off the heads of the old nails (called clenches) and levers the shoe off with pincers.

2 Next, he or she trims overgrown horn with hoof clippers and a drawing knife, and smooths off the edges with a large nail file called a rasp.

3 The farrier takes a shoe that is about the right size and holds it against the foot. It will probably need alterations to fit. This is done by placing it in a forge until the metal is red-hot and soft, and then pounding it into shape on an anvil. The hot shoe is carried with a pritchel.

4 While it is still hot, the shoe is tried on the foot. There is a lot of smoke, but it does not hurt the pony. The hot shoe leaves a burn mark on the horn which shows if it is sitting evenly and is the correct shape. Clips are made to keep the shoe in place on the foot — usually one on the front of a fore-shoe and two quarter clips on a hind-shoe.

5 More adjustments are made, if necessary. When a shoe is ready, it is cooled and fastened on the foot by driving nails through the hoof wall, where the pony has no feeling. The tips of the nails that stick out are turned over, clipped off, and hammered down. Usually four nails are used on the outside of the foot and three on the inside. The area toward the heel is left to allow for expansion as the pony moves.

6 The connection between the foot and the shoe is rasped smooth *(left)*.

IVEN all the right care and attention, your pony will be happy and healthy. But even the best looked-after pony might become ill or injure himself at some point. With some knowledgeable help, you may be able to deal with minor problems yourself. But, if you are in any doubt — and, always, in certain circumstances — send for the vet immediately, or something seemingly minor could quickly become a big problem. Knowing how your pony looks and behaves when he's feeling well, and recognizing the signs of a sick or unhealthy pony, means you can pick up on trouble quickly and know when to call the vet.

A well-cared-for, healthy pony has:

- ◆ A shine to his coat. But, remember, his thick winter fur is never going to really gleam.
- ◆ An interest in his surroundings, with ears flicking back and forth.
- ◆ A good appetite. Drinks regularly.
- ◆ Loose, supple skin, that is not tight.
- ◆ Good muscle tone — not fat, or thin with bones protruding.
- ◆ Moist, pink membranes in his eyes, nose, and mouth — these should not be pale or dry.

- ◆ Droppings that are not very hard or loose.
- ◆ Clear urine, passed regularly without strain.
- ◆ No puffiness or heat in the legs. Weight evenly distributed on all four feet.
- ◆ No cough, discharge from the nostrils, or swollen glands.
- ◆ Normal breathing and temperature.
- ◆ Bright eyes.

Pulse rate

THIS should be 36-42 beats per minute. Place two fingers (not your thumb) on the artery running inside the jaw, inside the foreleg, or behind the eye.

Temperature

NORMAL temperature is 100.4° F (38°C). It is taken by inserting a lubricated thermometer into the rectum for one minute. Call the vet if it is even one degree or more above or below.

MAKE a note of your pony's normal pulse and breathing rates so you can compare them if they change. Wait a while after exercise for readings to be accurate.

Breathing rate

THIS should be 8-12 breaths per minute. Watch the flanks of a pony at rest.

Healthy

Routine Health Care

Prevention is always better than a cure. There are three aspects of routine care that go a long way toward keeping your pony healthy and stopping potential problems in their tracks. These are worming and vaccination (shots) programs and routine teeth rasping.

WORMING

ALL horses and ponies carry internal parasites, called worms, in their stomachs. The parasites can never be eliminated completely because the pony eats the worm eggs with his grass all the time. But you can keep them under control with medication and good pasture management. If a pony is not wormed regularly, larvae grow inside his stomach and intestines. He'll lose weight and risk serious stomachache. A pony with worms will have a dull coat and be thin, with a potbelly.

◆ Worm regularly every six to eight weeks. You can get wormers from your vet or tack shop.
◆ Use either a paste in a syringe or powder given in the feed *(above)*. **Carefully follow the manufacturer's instructions regarding dosage.**
◆ Worm all ponies that share a field together at the same time.
◆ Make sure the brand you use deals with all types of parasites.
◆ Keep worms at bay by picking up droppings from the field every week.

SHOTS

PONIES are at risk from two serious, highly infectious diseases — tetanus and equine flu — that can be prevented by one simple vaccination by your vet.
Your pony will need a course of two shots, followed by yearly boosters. Both vaccinations can be given in one injection.

TEETH RASPING

PONIES' teeth grow all the time and get continuously worn down as the ponies chew their food. Trouble occurs because the grinding teeth at the back (the molars) often wear unevenly. This creates sharp edges that cut the sides of the mouth, especially when there is a bit in the mouth.
This can be very painful and, not surprisingly, causes riding problems. This situation can also keep the

pony from digesting food properly. Make sure your pony's teeth never cause problems by asking the vet to rasp them (file the edges off) every six months.

Common

WELL-CARED-FOR ponies, on the whole, stay fairly healthy, so there is no need to be alarmed by this list of common ailments. But knowing something about the various problems that can crop up will help you avoid them. And you can take the right steps if they do occur.

Thrush

IF YOU pick your pony's feet one day and find black, nasty-smelling stuff inside, the chances are he has thrush. This infection usually is caused by the pony standing around in wet and dirty bedding. Wash his feet thoroughly with an antiseptic scrub, then spray the sole with an antibiotic spray — and don't let it happen again. Keep his bedding and feet very clean!

ANY pain or discomfort in a pony's foot, leg, or joints could make him limp or go lame. Lameness is caused by injury or disease.

Sometimes lameness is very obvious, but, on other occasions, it might be very slight and barely noticeable. If your pony is lame, or you suspect he is, run your hand carefully down each leg feeling for any wound, heat, or swelling.

Pick up each foot, in turn, see if it feels hot, and look carefully for anything that might be stuck in the sole.

If you cannot find any obvious cause or if you are unsure which leg has the problem, ask someone knowledgeable to watch your pony move.

Jogging

A pony should walk taking rhythmical steps of the same length. If he does not, there is lameness in one or more legs.

Telltale signs of lameness

Lameness often does not show much in walk, so jog the pony away from the person watching, in a straight line. Turn the pony away from you (on your inside), then jog back and past your observer.

Do not hold the pony's head too closely, as the head position will help show which leg is sore.

If the pony is lame on a fore-leg, he will dip his head as his good foot goes down on the ground. If he is lame on a hind-leg, his quarters will dip more as his good foot goes down.

You may have spotted a wound, bump, or object in the foot. If so, it is time to use your first-aid skills *(see pages 48-49)*. But if the lameness is very severe or you have doubts about what is causing it, bring your pony inside and call the vet.

Ailments

Colic

COLIC is any kind of horse "tummyache," and it is very painful. For some reason, the pony is unable to digest his food properly because, somewhere along the line, there is a problem. As you know, the pony's insides are long and delicate, so colic is always serious. Call the vet immediately, and ask advice on how to deal with your pony until the vet arrives.

Any kind of feeding mistake can set off colic, though one of the most common causes is worm damage. Early warning signs include dullness of the coat, sweating, loss of appetite, a raised temperature, and restlessness, with the pony biting at or trying to kick his flanks. Do not let a pony with colic roll, even if he wants to, because he may suffer a fatal twisted gut.

Strangles

STRANGLES is a very infectious disease. It is uncommon, but it can be caught by young ponies, often from a new horse coming into a barn. The pony will look very ill and have very swollen throat glands. Isolate him in a comfortable stable, keep him warm, and call the vet.

Laminitis

PONIES are especially prone to this painful, crippling disease that can make them very lame, usually in both forefeet or both hind feet at the same time. It makes the pony stand leaning back like a rocking-horse.

It can occur when a pony is allowed to overindulge himself eating — that might mean eating too much grass, particularly the lush spring variety, or eating too much hard feed.

There are other causes that contribute to laminitis, such as a jarring from hard ground or a blood imbalance, but overfeeding is the usual cause — and so preventing this terrible condition is up to you! Don't let ponies and horses overeat, particularly in the spring and summer. Restrict their grazing if need be.

In laminitis, the joined layers of sensitive and insensitive laminae inside the foot split apart, making the main bone of the foot — the pedal bone — turn and drop downward, sometimes even through the sole. Laminitis is always very serious. If you suspect your pony is having an attack — usually signaled by a high temperature and difficulty in moving — stable him and call the vet immediately for treatment and advice on diet and care.

Common

If your pony has a tendency to cough, use dust-free bedding, such as shavings.

How to beat the cough

GO to any large barn in winter, and you are sure to hear one or more of the occupants coughing. All ponies will occasionally clear their throats with a cough, particularly when starting off a ride. But a persistent cough, or one accompanied by a runny nose, means trouble. It can soon wear a pony down.

Coughing can have many causes, but the two most common are infection and allergy. Infection may be a cold or equine flu, both of which cause a high temperature and fatigue and require a vet.

Mud fever

A SOGGY winter and a boggy field will put ponies at risk from cracked heels and mud fever. These are fungal infections that get into the skin when it becomes waterlogged and chapped or scratched. The telltale signs are that the skin becomes red and sore and then splits, or becomes scabby, causing painful sores.

Act on the first signs of mud fever or cracked heels before they get worse. You will need to trim back the hair and *carefully* pick off any scabs to let the air get to the skin. Now wash the legs gently with a medicated cleanser. Let them dry completely before rubbing in some zinc-based cream. Diaper rash creams are good for this. Keep the legs as dry as possible until the area is healed. If you can, keep the pony inside. But, if this is not possible, use a barrier cream like udder cream on the dry legs before turning him outside again.

Continually washing mud off legs in cold weather makes a pony likely to get mud fever. Wait for mud to dry, then brush it off. If you wash the legs, dry them before turning your pony out. Rain scald is a mud fever-type infection that affects the back during wet weather. Treat it in the same way — then give your pony better protection against the rain!

Ailments

Most cases of coughing are from the pony being sensitive to the dust and spores in hay and straw. This condition is called COPD — chronic obstructive pulmonary disease — and is very common.

The vet can give medication to help with serious cases, but, generally, this is a problem you can deal with yourself through incorporating some changes in your pony's management.

Basically, the pony needs as much fresh air as you can give him. If you can, turn him out regularly. If this is not possible, then let him spend as much time in the field as you can give him. When he has to come in, make sure he has a very airy, well-ventilated stable. Use dust-free bedding, such as shavings or paper. Replace hay with haylage, or soak the haynet for a few hours to allow the dust and spores to swell. Then they will not go into the pony's lungs.

Dampen all hard feed, too. Remember, it's no use taking all these precautions if the stable right next door has heaps of straw and hay in it.

Sweet itch

SWEET itch can make summer miserable for some ponies. They spend the whole time itching and scratching at the irritation on their manes and tails, often rubbing themselves bare. Because sweet itch probably is caused by an allergy to the bites of certain flies, the best way to avoid and treat it is to make sure the pony and insects do not meet.

Keep your pony inside at the worst time for gnats, in the morning and evening. At all times, put on lots of fly repellent and renew it frequently. Avoid putting a sweet-itch prone pony out into a field with a stream, river, pond, or ditch in it.

You can get benzyl benzoate lotion from your vet to help soothe your pony's itchy areas. In bad cases, the vet may prescribe something stronger.

ANY sick pony feels much like you do when you are ill — absolutely miserable. If your pony is ill, treat him as you would want to be treated. Make him comfortable, keep him warm, and do not bother him. Follow all your vet's instructions. Cut down on hard feed, and just give him hay. Replace his usual concentrates with a few handfuls of tasty chaff, apples, and carrots or a special mix for ill horses.

PERHAPS because they are big animals that move quickly and are easily frightened, ponies are always getting cuts and scrapes.

There are going to be times when your pony gets a cut or other injury. You can deal with minor injuries yourself with some basic first-aid knowledge. However small a cut or graze may seem, never ignore it because it can easily become infected.

Make a point of checking your pony over closely every day for cuts, particularly on his legs. Immediately clean and treat any injury you find.

First-

Step by Step

How to treat a wound

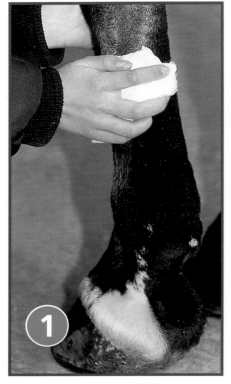

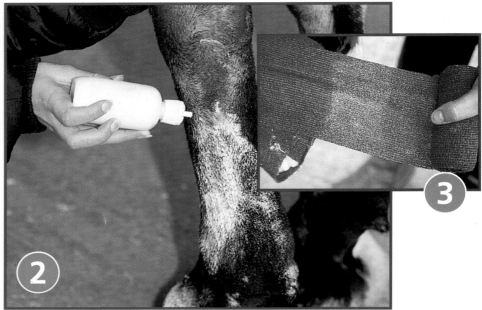

1 With a cotton pad and some clean, slightly salted water, clean the wound carefully. Let the water drip onto it first, then wipe it. Use a fresh piece of cotton with each wipe. Bruising and swelling can be reduced by some careful, gentle hosing.

2 Apply wound powder, or spray with antibiotic wound spray. Tiny cuts can be left uncovered but should be cleaned regularly until they heal.

3 Larger wounds or scrapes will need bandaging if they are in a place where you can bandage, such as the lower leg. Do not try to bandage other parts of the body. Keep the wounds clean.

4 If the wound is deep or more than 3/4 inch (2 cm) long, clean it as best you can. Then leave it alone, and call the vet. It may need stitches and antibiotics.

5 To stop bleeding, apply pressure to the wound with a clean gauze pad. If bleeding continues, apply a pad and a bandage. Then call the vet immediately.

Types of wounds

- Tear, such as on barbed wire.
- Lacerated, straightforward cut, such as on plain wire.
- Puncture, when the skin is pierced, such as stepping on a nail.
- Sores, caused by rubbing or chafing.
- Bruising, where the skin is not broken, but there is bleeding and swelling underneath.

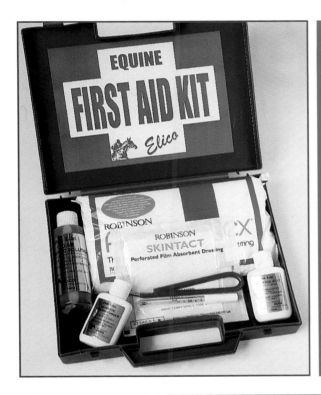

Get equipped

KEEP a well-stocked first-aid kit at the barn, and remember to take it to shows, too. You never know when you might need it.

It should contain:

- Thermometer
- Gauze bandages
- Scissors
- Safety pins or plaster tape
- Gauze pads
- Poultice
- Wound powder
- Roll of quilt bandages
- Antibiotic spray
- Dressings
- A bowl
- Roll of cotton

A PUNCTURE wound is especially dangerous because it is hard to see, but dirt and germs may have been forced deep into the skin and become trapped there. The infection has to be drawn out of the wound using a poultice. The most likely time you may need a poultice is if your pony steps on something sharp like a thorn, nail, or piece of glass that pierces his sole. He will be very lame. If there is infection inside, his foot will be hot and sore. If this happens:

1 Call your vet or farrier to come. He or she will find the spot and pare away some sole to release any infection building up inside.

2 Boil some water and allow it to cool to body temperature.

3 Cut your poultice to the right size — big enough to cover the whole area.

4 Put it on the foot (or other area) with the sticky side down.

5 Cover the entire foot with a plastic bag, plastic wrap, or an equiboot.

6 Bandage the plastic or equiboot securely. Then place it in another bag, and secure it with a bandage.

REMEMBER — Poultices must be changed twice a day. Use them for at least two days after your pony has healed and there is no more discharge.

IF you find a sore or saddle gall on your pony, where his tack has been rubbing, it is human error. Properly fitted tack on a clean pony should never cause him discomfort like this.

- Check your tack and get advice about how it is fitted. Do not use it again until you are sure it fits correctly. Keep tack clean and supple, and always brush your pony in the areas where his tack goes before riding.
- Do not ride until the sores have healed. Clean the area, and spray with antiseptic.

THE bridle is a set of straps that fasten around the pony's head and support the bit in his mouth. The reins, attached to the rings of the bit, are your communication lines with your pony. The bit sits over the tongue in the gap between the pony's front and back teeth. Most bits are made of stainless steel, although the mouthpiece is sometimes rubber or plastic. There are many kinds of bits, and each type works in a slightly different way. Most ponies wear a simple snaffle bit, with or without a joint in the center. It might have loose rings, that slide through the mouthpiece, or fixed eggbutt rings. Stronger ponies may need a curb bit with a curb chain, such as a Pelham. Do not change your bit without asking the advice of your instructor.

TACK, or saddlery, is the name given to all the gear a pony wears when he is ridden. Every rider needs to learn about the different items of tack, how they fit, and why a pony has them. Each has a special use, but the two main pieces of equipment every pony wears are a saddle and a bridle. To be safe, effective, and comfortable for you and your pony, all tack must fit well and be put on properly every time you ride.

Tack:

You cannot use just any bit on your pony. His bit must fit him well if it is to work properly and not hurt his mouth. When the bridle is on and the bit is at the right height, there should be just a small part of the mouthpiece showing between his lips and the bit-ring (just enough to fit your finger in).

Step by Step

1 If you are not in the stable, fasten the halter around the pony's neck.

2 Facing forward, stand close to the pony's near (left) side, and put the reins over his head. Hold the bridle so the bit is in front of his mouth, then guide it in with your left hand. If this is awkward, you may have to slip your thumb into the side of the gums, where there aren't any teeth, to encourage him to open up.

How to put on a bridle ...

3 Carefully bring the head-piece up over the ears, one at a time. Then pull out the forelock and straighten the mane. Check to see that the bit is at a comfortable height. It should just wrinkle the lips, as if the pony is smiling. It must not be too low and droopy so it knocks on the teeth, or too high and tight. You can adjust it using the cheekpieces.

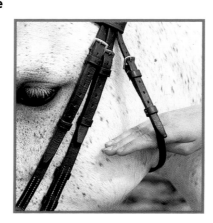

4 Buckle the throat-lash, making sure that four fingers will easily fit between the pony's cheek and the strap. Check that the noseband is lying underneath the cheekpieces and is sitting level, midway between the pony's cheekbones and the bit. Fasten the noseband snugly, but leave space for two fingers to slip underneath. Make sure all the straps are securely in their "keepers."

The Bridle & Bit

Parts of the bridle

... and how to take it off

1 Undo the throat-lash and noseband.
2 Ease the headpiece over the ears. Gently slip the bit out, taking care not to bang the teeth.
3 Put on the pony's halter, then bring the reins over his head.

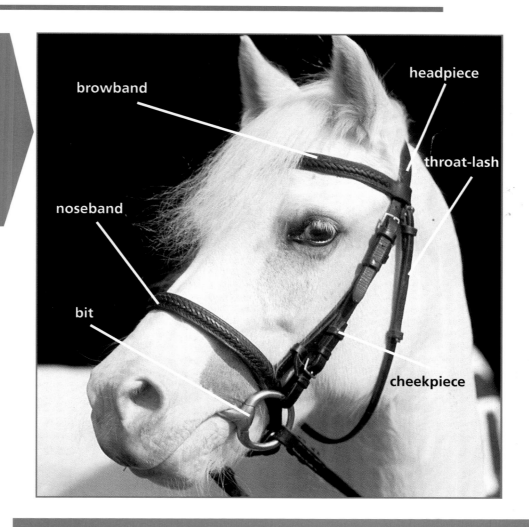

browband
headpiece
throat-lash
noseband
bit
cheekpiece

The Noseband

MOST bridles have an ordinary cavesson noseband that sits above the bit *(above)*. It is possible to gain extra control over a pony that tries to open his mouth to avoid the action of the bit by using a "drop" type of noseband that fits below the bit.

This could either be a traditional drop noseband, a Flash noseband made up of a cavesson plus a drop strap, or a crossed or figure-eight noseband.

If you use a dropped noseband of any kind, make sure it fits, so it does not squeeze on the soft part of the pony's nose and hamper his breathing. Fasten it snugly, but not crunchingly tight, making sure the pony's lips are not pinched.

1

THE saddle is what keeps you sitting securely on your pony's back in the right position. Then you can give the aids with your legs in the correct place on his sides and stay in balance as he moves. There are several different kinds of special saddles designed for particular activities. For everyday riding, you will use a general purpose one.

Saddles were traditionally always made of leather, but it is now possible to choose between leather and synthetic saddles. Synthetics are very lightweight, tough, easy to clean, and cost less. All saddles are built around a wooden or plastic frame called a tree. The tree's cushioned panels help place your weight evenly, making it easier for your pony to carry you.

The stirrups are not attached to the saddle but hang by straps, called the leathers, from the bars of the tree, under the skirt. The girth, which can be made of leather, cotton, or webbing, fits around the pony's belly to hold everything in place. A fitted pad is a saddle-shaped pad that fits underneath the saddle for extra comfort and to absorb sweat.

Tack:

Saddle fit

GETTING a good-fitting saddle for your pony is crucial. A bad fit can do a lot of damage to a pony's back. It is worth taking time to make sure it fits well. Don't presume that any saddle will fit any pony because ponies come in all shapes and sizes. If your new pony comes with a saddle, it may not necessarily fit because, even if it once did, ponies can change shape.

Ask a professional saddler to fit the pony with a saddle. You may not need to buy a new one — or the old one might just need restuffing by the saddler. When buying a new saddle, always have it fitted to the pony first.

Here are some checks to see if your saddle is OK for your pony, or if it may need restuffing or replacing. All saddles do need restuffing from time to time.

◆ When it is in the right place on the pony's back, the saddle should sit evenly — not high at the front or at the back. It should not move around a lot as the pony moves (although there will be some movement).

◆ With a rider on board, there should still be plenty of daylight visible all the way along the gullet, front to back. You should be able to fit four fingers easily into the gullet at the front and have at least three fingers' width at the back. The gullet should be wide enough to sit on either side of the withers. You need to be able to get your fingers under the padding quite easily — if it is tight, it will pinch.

◆ Check for a broken tree, too. Hold the saddle with the pommel in your lap, and use both hands to pull the cantle towards you. There should be only the tiniest amount of give due to springiness built into the tree. If it creaks or really moves, the tree is broken and is no good.

◆ Lumpy or very soft panels mean it's time for restuffing.

1 IF you are not in a stable, tie your pony up or have someone hold him. Hold the saddle with your left hand on the pommel and your right hand under the seat. Standing on the near (left) side, place the saddle gently on the highest part of the withers.

Step by Step

How to put on a saddle

2 NOW slide the saddle down to the correct position. Pull the fitted pad up into the gullet.

Saddles

3 GO around the front of the pony to the other side and let the girth down. Back on the near side, take the girth from under the belly, ensuring there are no twists. Then buckle it up to the girth straps beneath the saddle flaps — gently! You will have to tighten it up later because most ponies puff themselves out at first. Use either the first two straps or outside two.

4 PULL down the buckle guard. Take each foreleg, one at a time, and pull forward to ease out any wrinkles under the girth. Run the stirrups down the leathers only when you are ready to ride.

Taking it off ...

1 Make sure the stirrup irons are run up. Undo the girth on the near side.

2 Go around to the off side, and put the girth up over the saddle.

3 Back on the near side, lift the saddle well clear of the pony's back. Put the saddle down carefully, somewhere safe. Rub the pony's back to help get the circulation going again.

Martingales

Tack:
Carry it properly

ANOTHER piece of tack your pony might wear is called a martingale. This is a neck strap with other straps running from it to the bridle or reins and to the girth. Martingales keep the pony from throwing his head up so high, which makes riding difficult.

A running martingale divides into two straps with a ring on each end, through which each rein is threaded. To keep it in position, it should always be used with rubber stops in front of the rings on the reins, and one where the straps join at the chest. It must fit right, or it will either be of no use at all or it will restrict the pony too much. Free the reins, and hold the martingale straps up toward the pony's withers. They should reach to about a hand's width away.

A standing martingale *(above)* has one broad strap that fastens directly to a cavesson noseband (never to a drop-type noseband). For the right fit, push the strap up into the pony's gullet. It should comfortably go up to the throat-lash.

YOUR tack, and especially your saddle, is the most expensive equipment you own — besides the pony himself. If you take good care of your saddlery, it will last years. But it is very easily damaged, and damaged tack can be unsafe for you and your pony. Carry it as shown *(at left)*.

Hints

NOT many pony owners like cleaning tack, but it's a necessary chore that must be done at least once a week. Cleaning after every ride would be the best. It is important to clean tack regularly because grease soon builds up on it, which can cause rubs and sores on your pony's skin. Grease and dirt also make the stitching rot, making the tack unsafe. Leather that is hardly ever soaped gets stiff and cracked and could break at any time.

Keeping your tack clean

THIS quick clean takes just a few minutes. Do a more complete job once a week when you will need to take all the pieces apart and clean them thoroughly.

Step by Step

1 HANG up the bridle to clean it. Put the saddle on a saddle stand *(right)* or over your knee.

2 EQUIP yourself with a small bucket of clean, warm water, some saddle soap, a cloth, and a few sponges. An old toothbrush is handy for scrubbing the bit, stirrup irons, and treads.

3 USE the cloth to wipe the bit and stirrup irons. Rinse the cloth, and wipe all the leatherwork on both sides, making sure you remove all the grease you can see. Tough spots (called jockeys) may need to be scratched with a fingernail. Don't get the leather too wet.

4 NOW dip the saddle soap in the water. Rub it into the sponge, trying not to make too much lather. Soap the leather all over with the sponge. Finish with a final polish from a soft, dry cloth.

TIP

IF your leather tack gets wet, never put it by the fire or radiator. Let it dry out naturally, or it will crack and break.

5 DON'T forget your cotton girth and fitted pad — there's nothing nastier for your pony than having to keep wearing the same greasy, sweaty ones. It is easy to pop these in a washing machine. You can prevent wear and tear on the machine from buckles by putting the girth in an old pillowcase. Nylon halters and lightweight stable blankets can be washed in a machine, too.

6 NO excuses if you have synthetic tack, which is very easy to clean. Simply wipe any greasy patches with a damp cloth containing diluted liquid detergent.

Riders need to recognize different boots and know how to use them.

Boots

Protection pointers

THERE are times when your pony's legs need some protection. This could be when you are jumping because he may get a bump. Or, perhaps, his action brings his legs a bit too close together and he knocks into himself. At these times, boots are used to guard the pony's legs. Riders need to know how to recognize the different types of boots and their uses. The most common riding boots are:

Brushing boots

FOR: Exercise, jumping, especially cross-country.
FIT: Around the lower leg, fastened snugly but not too tightly. You should be able to place a finger in between. Always fasten with the straps on the outside, pointing backward. Front boots usually have four straps, and hind boots have five straps.

Bell boots

FOR: Ponies that overstep with their hind feet, catching the heels of the forefeet.
FIT: On the forefeet only. Some fit around the pastern and are tied with a strap (not too tightly). Rubber boots need to be pulled on over the hoof. You might need a hoof pick or piece of rope to get them on and off.

Tendon boots

FOR: Showjumping or for exercise if the pony is likely to strike into himself high up.
FIT: Used on forelegs only. The padded section of the boot sits around tendons at the back of the lower leg. The straps go around the front, fastening on the outside, pointing backward.

& Bandages

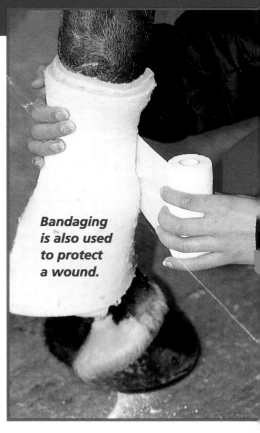

Bandaging is also used to protect a wound.

LEG protection can have other purposes, too. Some competition riders use polo bandages to guard and support their horses' tendons during work. Another kind of bandaging, using stable bandages, can be used to keep a sick or tired horse's legs warm and supported in the stable, for protection during traveling, or to keep on a dressing over a wound or injury. Bandaging is, therefore, a useful skill for you to learn — although don't expect to do a perfect job the first time!

Exercise bandages are narrow gauze bandages put on from under the knee or hock to just above the fetlock. Putting on exercise bandages properly is a very skilled job. Badly placed bandages could damage your pony's legs. If you want to give your pony extra leg protection during riding, shows, and competitions, it is better to be on the safe side and use brushing boots. When you are near your pony's feet, always squat, never kneel or sit down — you may need to move in a hurry!

Stable bandages are wide bandages made from a soft, stretchy material like felt or wool. They are put on snugly, but not tightly, over padding, from below the knee or hock, over the fetlock, around the pastern, and up again.

Check List

1 ALWAYS use padding underneath any bandage. This can either be synthetic padding or a piece of quilt bandage cut off a roll. Make sure it is the right size and is lying smoothly on the leg.

2 HAVE your bandage tightly rolled up, ready. Start as pictured *(above)*, then wind around, tucking in the flap with the next wind. Each turn should cover two thirds of the previous one.

3 WHEN you reach the bottom, bandage upward again. Finish halfway up the leg if you can.

4 FASTEN the bandage firmly. It might have Velcro or tapes that need tying. With tapes, do a double bow on the outside of the leg, never the front or back. Tuck in the ends. Make fasteners snug but not so tight that they dig in.

5 CAN you easily slip a finger inside the bandage? If not, it is too tight, so try again.

6 ALWAYS bandage the legs in pairs — not just one foreleg or back leg. Even if only one is injured, the other leg will need a bandage for support.

Things you need to keep your pony safe

Travel boots

Special padded boots to guard against knocks or your pony stepping on himself. Stable bandages can be used instead.

Tail bandage

Keeps the pony from leaning on the ramp and rubbing his tail raw.

Light blanket

This is secured with a padded roller, to which the tail guard fastens. In hot weather, a cool, thin blanket protects against dust, flies, and knocks. If your pony is sweaty or might get hot and sweaty, put an anti-sweat sheet underneath, then the other blanket on top. Fold back the front of the top blanket and secure everything under the roller. This will keep him warm but also keep him from overheating.

Extras

Extras include: A poll guard that fits on the halter behind the ears in case the pony throws his head up and bumps it, bell boots, and knee and hock boots (fasten tightly above the knee/hock and loosely underneath, to protect these joints).

EVEN if you do not go to shows or rallies very often, there are going to be times when your pony needs to be transported in a trailer or stall box. Traveling can be a risky and stressful time for a pony, but you can make it safer and easier for him by equipping him with protective gear. Know how to load, transport, and unload him properly.

Hints

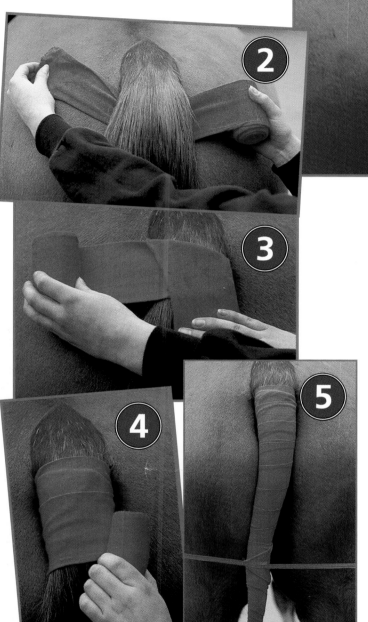

Putting on the perfect tail bandage

BESIDES their use in traveling, tail bandages can be applied after grooming or any time that you want to keep your pony's tail clean and neat. Remember not to leave a tail bandage on too long — a few hours will do.

1 Brush the top of the tail with a damp water brush.

2 Stand slightly to one side of your pony's tail. Lift it gently and place a few inches (cm) of narrow polo-type bandage underneath.

3 Wind around once tightly. Tuck in the flap, and wind around again, keeping the bandage flat and firm.

4 Now start winding down the tail, keeping an even pressure and covering a half to two-thirds of the previous turn each time.

5 Stop when you reach the end of the tailbone. Now start going up the tail. Finish halfway back up. Wind the tapes a few times around the tail firmly, then tie in a double bow. Tuck in the ends.

6 Bend the tail gently back into its natural shape.

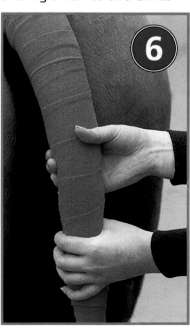

Taking it off...

TO take a tail bandage off, simply undo the tapes, take hold of the top of the bandage, and firmly pull it downward.

ALWAYS give yourself plenty of time for loading, especially with a pony that is not used to traveling. If you think about it, walking into an enclosed space is quite a frightening experience for a pony. So you need to be patient and give him confidence. If everyone keeps calm, you should not have too many problems.

Loading tips

1 RECRUIT at least one, and preferably two, helpers who are confident with horses.

2 MAKE the trailer as inviting as you can. Open any front doors to let the light in, and have some straw or shavings on the floor. You can put some on the ramp, too. Hang up a haynet securely.

3 POSITION the trailer alongside a wall. Have your pony suited up and ready to travel. Wear your riding hat and gloves and some sensible boots or shoes.

4 LEAD your pony straight to the center of the ramp. Do not drag him along behind.

5 WALK just ahead of him into the trailer. Get a helper to immediately fasten the breech straps behind him and carefully put up the ramp. Now tie the lead-rope to the string on the tie ring. Give him enough rope to move his head up and down and reach the haynet easily, but not so much that he could try to turn around in a trailer with no partition.

6 NEVER transport two ponies in a trailer without a central partition. Never get inside the trailer when it is moving, and never place yourself down alongside your pony in a partitioned trailer at any time. If he panics, you will be trapped and injured.

MOST ponies that have never had a bad experience traveling will load well. However, some may be frightened or uncooperative about loading. Keep calm, and try these tips:

◆ Load another pony first into the other side of a partitioned trailer. This might give him confidence that all is well.

◆ Put a bucket of food inside, just out of reach, but do not give him any until he has stepped onto the ramp. Then make him step forward for more. Try not to stand right in front of him with the bucket, as you will be blocking his way.

◆ If your pony just calmly stands at the base of the ramp, pick up one of his feet and put it down on the ramp.

◆ If all else fails, lunge lines usually do the trick. Take two lines and clip one end of each to string loops on either side of the back of the trailer. Your two helpers need to walk past each other, crossing their lines behind the pony, keeping the lines up over the hocks. Then they can slowly close the lines in, encouraging the pony forward.

Hints

Towing tips for parents

◆ Make sure your towing vehicle can handle the weight it has to pull.

◆ The trailer must be regularly serviced.

◆ When you hitch up, double check that the safety chain is over the towbar, the brake is off, the coupling is on correctly, and that all the electric hook-ups work.

◆ Drive very slowly and carefully, especially around corners and when circling. Imagine you don't want to spill a cup of coffee on the dashboard. Allow plenty of room for turns.

◆ Give yourself time and space to brake slowly.

◆ If you are carrying just one pony in a partitioned trailer, load him into the "inside" side. He can balance better there and will not be bumping along.

Reluctant ones

Unloading

IF your trailer has a front-unload door, untie the pony. Then undo the breast bar and slowly lead him out forward. Keep his head down. If you are transporting only a short way, your pony can be in his tack. But always put a blanket on top, and make sure the stirrups are up and that the reins are threaded up out of the way through the bridle throat-lash. Use a halter over the bridle for tying up and leading. The pony should be wearing travel boots.

With a rear-unload trailer, untie the pony and have a helper lower the ramp gently. Undo the breech straps. Make your pony stand for a few seconds before "asking" him to step slowly backward down the ramp, with you at his head, keeping him straight.

Glossary

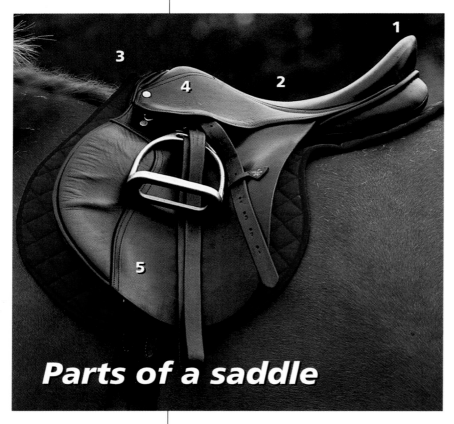

Parts of a saddle

1. Cantle
2. Seat
3. Pommel
4. Skirt
5. Saddle flap

action — the way a horse or pony moves.

bit — the piece of the bridle that is held in the pony's mouth, usually made of metal. The reins are attached to the bit. They are the rider's means of giving hand aids to the pony.

cantle — the back of the saddle.

cavesson — 1) A simple type of noseband. 2) Special headgear with a ring fixed to the noseband, to which a lunging rein is attached.

chaff — straw, or a mixture of hay and straw, chopped up and added to feed to provide extra fiber.

clench — the part of a nail that is left sticking up out of the hoof wall after a farrier puts a horseshoe on a horse or pony. He/she then bends the nail over and hammers the end down.

clip — 1) Shearing off part of a horse or pony's winter coat to keep the animal cool during work. 2) The part of a horseshoe that turns over the edge of the foot to keep the shoe in place.

colic — a horse or pony stomachache.

dock — the solid, top part of a horse or pony's tail, where the bone lies.

drop noseband — a type of noseband that fits below the bit.

eggbutt — a *T*-shaped joint between the mouthpiece and rings of a bit that stops the animal's lips from being pinched.

farrier — a professional trained to care for and fit shoes on a horse or pony's feet.

feed bucket — a trough in a stable used for feeding.

fitted pad — a cotton or fleece pad under a saddle that eases pressure and absorbs sweat.

frog — the rubbery, *V*-shaped structure in the center of the sole on the foot of a horse or pony.

gall — a sore around a horse or pony's belly caused by a girth that is dirty or pinching the skin.

halter — headgear made of a noseband, headpiece, and throat-lash. Used for leading and tying up.

haylage — grass that has been cut and baled into sealed bags when partly dry.

horse — a large hoofed animal of the Equidae family that is over 14.2 hands high. A hand equals 4 inches (10.2 centimeters).

keepers — the small leather loops that hold the ends of the bridle straps neatly in place.

lame — when an ill or injured horse or pony cannot move without feeling discomfort.

laminitis — a painful disease that makes the feet of a horse or pony very tender.

loading — putting a horse or pony into a trailer.

loose ring — a kind of joint on a bit where the rings are not fixed to the mouthpiece but can slip through it.

manure — recycled natural material that fertilizes the soil.

martingale — a neckstrap attached between the forelegs to the girth and also the reins or noseband to give the rider more control of a horse or pony.

microbes — microorganisms or germs.

near side — the left-hand side of a horse or pony.

New Zealand blanket — a tough blanket for outdoor use.

off side — the right-hand side of a horse or pony.

picking out — cleaning out a horse or pony's hooves.

pommel — the front of a saddle.

pony — a large hoofed animal of the Equidae family that is under 14.2 hands high. A hand equals 4 inches (10.2 cm).

predator — an animal that survives by hunting other animals.

pulling — thinning out a thick mane or tail by taking out just a few hairs at a time.

regurgitate — to bring back up incompletely digested stomach contents.

roller — a wide strap used around the belly to keep a blanket in place on a horse or pony.

saddle stand — a frame on which a saddle sits for storage or cleaning.

saddlery — saddles and other gear for horses and ponies.

snaffle — the largest and most commonly seen family of bits, usually with one ring on either side of the mouthpiece.

stirrup — a metal ring that hangs on a strap from a saddle. It supports a rider's foot.

supplement — an object that completes or adds to something.

surcingle — a narrow, stretchy strap that is placed over a saddle in cross-country competitions for extra security or placed around the belly to fasten a blanket.

tack — stable gear or harness equipment, such as a saddle and bridle, used on a horse or pony.

tendon — tough tissue that connects muscles to bones. In horses and ponies, the main tendons run down the back of the cannon bones in the lower legs.

tree — the frame that a saddle is built around.

turning out — letting a horse or pony loose into a field.

ventilation — a circulation of fresh and healthy air.

vermin — small animals, such as lice or fleas, that can do harm.

worms — internal parasites carried by all horses and ponies. Infestation can make a horse or pony very ill unless controlled by regular doses of a wormer.

Care for your horse or pony, and he will care for you!

For Further Study

Books

First Aid for Horses. Tim Hawcroft (Crescent Books)

Horse and Pony Care. Tim Hawcroft (Crescent Books)

Horses. Animal Families (series). Hans D. Dossenbach (Gareth Stevens)

Magnificent Horses of the World (series). T. Mícek & H.J. Schrenk (Gareth Stevens)

The Man Who Listens to Horses. Monty Roberts (Random House)

The Nature of Horses. Stephen Budiansky (The Free Press)

The Riding Book. Ginny L. Winter (Astor-Honor)

The Saddle Club (series). Bonnie Bryant (Gareth Stevens)

The Ultimate Horse. Elwyn Hartley Edwards (Dorling Kindersley)

A Very Young Rider. Jill Krementz (Dell)

With the Wind. Liz Damrell (Orchard)

Videos

Basic Horse Care. (Visual Education Productions)

Basic Horsemanship: Health Care. (Visual Education Productions)

Daily Grooming. (Edmar Video Productions)

Emergency First Aid. (Discovery Trail)

Equine Nutrition. (Discovery Trail)

Feeding Horses. (Visual Education Productions)

For the Love of Animals: Basic Horse Care and Ownership. (GCG Productions)

Grooming Your Horse. (RMI Media)

Horses: To Care Is to Love. (AIMS Media)

Stefanie Powers: Introduction to Horse Care. (Paramount Home Video)

Web Sites

netvet.wustl.edu/horses.htm

www.cowgirls.com/dream/jan/rodeo.htm

www.freerein.com/haynet/

www.horse-country.com/

www.horseadvice.com/

Index